7/39

**Knowing
Contentment,
Peace and
Fulfillment—
NOW**

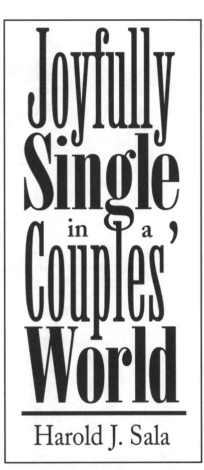

Joyfully Single in a Couples' World

Harold J. Sala

HORIZON BOOKS

CAMP HILL, PENNSYLVANIA

HORIZON BOOKS

3825 Hartzdale Drive
Camp Hill, PA 17011
www.christianpublications.com

Joyfully Single in a Couples' World
ISBN: 0-88965-142-6

Printed in the United States of America

02 03 04 05 06   7 6 5 4 3

Unless otherwise indicated,
Scripture taken from the HOLY BIBLE:
NEW INTERNATIONAL VERSION ®.
© 1973, 1978, 1984 by the International Bible Society.
Used by permission of Zondervan Bible Publishers.

Scripture labeled "TLB" is taken from The Living Bible, copyright
1971 by Tyndale House Publishers, Wheaton, IL;
Scripture labeled "KJV" is taken from the HOLY BIBLE: King
James Version; Scripture labeled "NASB" is taken from the New
American Standard Bible, copyright by The Lockman Foundation
1960, 1962, 1963, 1971, 1972, 1973, 1975.

The use of selected references from various versions of the Bible in
this publication does not necessarily imply endorsement of the
versions in their entirety by either the publisher or the author.

Contents

Foreword

I heard it said once: "Your circumstances may not immediately change, but your attitude can change, and that makes all the difference in the world." This book is about making the decision to have joy in your life no matter what your circumstances.

Susan is a hero of mine. Her love for life and God is contagious. Yet her circumstances haven't always been positive. As a teenager, Susan rebelled against her family and her faith and made some admittedly unwise decisions about relationships.

As a single adult she came across this famous passage of Scripture: "Do not be anxious about anything, but in everything, by prayer and petition, with thanksgiving, present your requests to God. And the peace of God, which transcends all understanding, will guard your hearts and your minds in Christ Jesus" (Philippians 4:6-7).

Susan is a determined person and she decided to go after that joy and not wait for it to "just happen." Susan made a commitment to give over her anxiety to God daily, pray with thanksgiving in her heart and see what would happen in her life. None of her circumstances changed immediately, but she found herself experiencing joy in her life because she had made better proactive decisions about what to do with her relationship with God and others. Today, Susan is a radiant person with a joy that runs deep.

You will see in Dr. Sala's wonderful book that joy is a choice. It comes from making wise decisions about your life and your future. But the decisions can't be made in the future; they must be made today to bring joy for tomorrow. You will learn practical wisdom as you follow the principles in *Joyfully Single in a Couples' World*.

Recently, Susan got married. I asked her how it felt to finally receive her heart's desire, which had been eluding her for such a very long time. I believe her answer is worth repeating: "I'm glad I found my peace with God and made better decisions before I got married. If not, I would have brought all my 'stuff' into the marriage and I would still be looking for joy. The peace I have found in my life has more to do with my relationship with God than my marriage."

Dr. Sala is truly one of the wisest people I know, and the advice you will receive will make an eternal benefit in your life. In these pages he doesn't offer fairy tale answers, but rather a "let's roll up our sleeves and get to work on our issues" kind of material. He will challenge you on every page to dare to dream and dare to become the person of your dreams. With God's help, and by making the right decisions, you truly can live joyfully as a single in a couples' world!

Go for it!

Jim Burns, Ph.D
President, National Institute of Youth Ministry

Introduction

There is a growing segment of society which is often taken for granted. Generally unappreciated and often misunderstood, this army of talented men and women represents more diversity of opinions, lifestyles and backgrounds than any other group today. These men and women, I believe, constitute our most significant and misunderstood minority—single men and women.

At the onset of this book, I want to make it clear that this is not a clinical book *about* singles, analyzing and defining them as a strange phenomenon created by the growing hesitation of men and women to assume the responsibilities of married life, cataloging their idiosyncracies as a scientist would who studies aardvarks somewhere in a remote corner of the world. This is a book written *to* and *for* singles.

Apart from being single myself before God brought the wonderful girl into my life who eventually became my wife, I have been counseling and working with people—many of whom are single—for more than thirty-five years. When I began doing family seminars in the 1970s, we began to realize that most conferences were directed to only part of the body of Christ—those who were married. Repeatedly as I traveled and spoke I met with singles, some of whom were the most angry and frustrated individuals I have ever worked with. They often expressed feelings of neglect, irritation and outright anger with God and certainly others who constantly diagnosed their loneliness and then attempted to "cure" their singleness by introducing them to someone they didn't want to meet.

I then began to address the needs of singles, producing seminars and written materials, but more often listening and loving them. Then I attempted to help pastors, administrators and leaders understand some of the unique needs of singles and give them the respect which they deserve as God's children.

As I sat at breakfast discussing *Joyfully Single in a Couples' World* with my son, who was, at age thirty-one, single and enjoying life, Steve asked (suspiciously), "Dad, what's going to be the bottom line of your book?"

Taking a moment to collect my thoughts I replied, "Steve, what I want to accomplish is to help singles understand that they can find contentment and peace where they are right now, that they don't have to be married to be happy. I want to help them come to grips with who they are and to help them to discover where God wants them to go with their lives and futures." Finding God's help to meet the present need is the key to peace and fulfillment.

"If I were only married, I'd be happy," is a phrase which I've heard over and over again. It reflects wishful thinking. If you are unhappy as a single, marriage isn't going to change your outlook, but it may magnify it. Some of you who are single wish you were married, but a lot of the married folks I know wish they were single. Contentment is a choice, a decision which you make and can be realized whether single or married.

OK, you're single, but there's one thing for sure: It's a couples' world—or at least, that's what most married folks think. A lot of them believe that they, being the majority, are in control, and they often let you know that by not including you in couples functions such as dinner parties, holiday events and sometimes even family gatherings. Society tends to box and label individuals with the wedding altar as the continental divide between married and single.

Thinking they are funny, insensitive individuals make sarcastic comments like, "What's the matter with you that you aren't married?" (The next time you hear that try responding with, "What's the matter with you that you aren't single?") Or they generously offer to play the role of matchmaker—something which singles universally detest. "I'd be glad to introduce you to my cousin" (whom you met once before, distinctly remembering that his buck teeth protrude enough to eat corn on the cob through a tennis racket).

You want to say, "Forget it! I can handle my social life without your assistance," but you don't. Instead you burn inside and seethe with anger and resentment.

Though some churches have established programs of ministry designed to help meet the spiritual and social needs of singles, a lot of churches are not sure what to do with singles apart from inviting them to work in the nursery or teach a Sunday school class. Many churches have few if any functions specifically geared to singles. Their response to the diverse needs of singles is a generic class often taught by a middle-aged single who, if the truth were known, is looking over the eligibles himself. The one study group that exists consists of participants ranging in age from "just out of college" to senior seniors in their eighties whose mates have beaten them to glory!

Joe Bailey, in an article entitled "Saved, Single, and Second-Class," voiced the feelings of so many when he wrote, "I have trouble with church leaders (and congregations) considering single people some kind of strange species that they do not know what to do with."[1]

It is high time that we stopped thinking of families only in terms of couples, considering singles to be an anomaly (something must be wrong when you get into your thirties and aren't married!) or undeveloped appendages which need to be nurtured and brought into maturity in marriage.

I suppose that I am certifying the obvious when I write this, but I've gotta do it anyway: Jesus Christ was single all of His life, and He lived and functioned in a couples' world not unlike ours today. Though He grew up in a family with at least seven siblings (half-brothers and sisters) and was entertained in the homes of families, Jesus neither spoke disparagingly of the single life nor glorified the importance of being married. In Matthew's Gospel, there is a discussion dealing with marriage and divorce when Jesus somewhat matter-of-factly spoke of the marriage relationship affirming that it had been this way since the days of Adam and Eve.

Hearing the words of Jesus, the disciples responded, "If that is how it is, it is better not to marry!" And Jesus replied, "Not everyone can accept this statement. . . . Some are born without the ability to marry, and some are disabled by men, and some refuse to marry for the sake of the Kingdom of Heaven. Let anyone who can, accept my statement" (Matthew 19:10-12, TLB).

As Barb Sroka put it: "Our Lord was not married. He is also the one we are commanded to emulate. Jesus spoke often of the lusts of the flesh, but seldom of the advantages or disadvantages of paired or unpaired living."

The second part of my disclaimer is that the individuals who impacted the world of the first century for God—such as Paul, Stephen, Mark and Timothy—were noticeably single. Consider the impact of the tentmaker turned rabbi who contributed more to the theological development of the early Church and certainly to the New Testament than any other person. Paul was single when he penned the thirteen letters which bear his name. I, for one, believe that Paul had been married at one time and then became widowed. According to tradition, Paul was a member of the Sanhedrin. To belong to this august body, it was necessary for a male to be at least twenty years of age and *married*. Furthermore, the insights which Paul made regarding marriage and family living seemingly reflect the views of one who had been there, who had experienced both the joys and frustrations of married life.

Joyfully Single in a Couples' World is written with the prayer and expectation that God will help you to find contentment and fulfillment where you are now, for contentment is not a destination but a journey.

One last comment before we go further. Marriage is a beautiful relationship which was instituted by God Himself in the Garden. It isn't an appendage tacked on to the model of creation; it was at the very heart of what God wills for most people. *But marriage is not for everyone!* Nor did God intend that everyone find his or her "perfect ten" and settle down as a couple and have children.

Some individuals find their greatest fulfillment in marriage; some find the same thing in the solitude of singleness. Some who are married would struggle with singleness while some who are single could not cope with the expectations and pressures of married life. But there is one thing that is certain: Whether you are single or married, you can find contentment, peace and fulfillment.

Putting a gold band on your wedding finger or saying "I do" at a marriage altar doesn't make you a whole, complete individual. You are that already! Single or married, you are an individual who is unique, made in the image of God. This you must affirm and never forget. You can live joyfully as a single in a couples' world. That's the message of this book.

Endnote

1. Joe Bailey, "Saved, Single, and Second-Class," *Eternity* (March 1983), p. 23.

1

Making Peace with Your Dreams

"If my life is bound by the poles of birth and death, if my life has no eternal significance, then why not grab whatever pleasure I can squeeze out of my brief time on earth?"[1]

—*R.C. Sproul*

So you're single. How do you as a single respond to the realities of living in a couples' world? What word or phrase would best describe the way you feel?

__ Content
__ On the look
__ Angry
__ Resentful
__ Annoyed
__ Disappointed
__ Frustrated
__ Inadequate
__ Lonely
__ Bypassed
__ Afraid
__ Neglected
__ Miserable
__ Hopeful
__ Expectant
__ Misled

For each one of you who is unmarried, there is a married couple. That means you are outnumbered. I don't know whether majority rule carries the day, but I know for a fact it does in the thinking of married couples because it is still a couples' world. That doesn't mean you like it that way. You don't! When I ask singles to describe their greatest frustration, at the top of the list is the way they are treated in a couples' world.

As much as I would like to tell you things are changing and people are becoming more sensitive and caring, I don't see much evidence of it! Old cliques and attitudes change very slowly.

At the same time, the ranks of you who are single are growing and growing and growing as the world is getting younger. In China, fifty percent of the population is twenty-seven years of age or younger. In the Philippines, fifty percent of the population is twenty years of age or younger, which means that soon, if not already, there will be more singles than marrieds.

At the present time forty percent of all adults in the United States are single, and according to researcher George Barna, "At some point early in the next century, the majority of Americans will be single."[2]

It is also true that couples are putting off marriage longer and longer. Presently, the median age for you who are female is 24.5 years of age. For you men, it is 26.5 years of age. Men and women are marrying four years later than did their parents a generation ago.

Recently Guidelines (my ministry organization) did a poll of over 1,000 singles. While the vast majority of those who responded expected to marry at some time in the future, most were awaiting the knight in shining armor who would come sweeping into their lives and carry them away or were waiting to be blown away by the beautiful young thing who would cause their hearts to palpitate.

Everyone, of course, is not sitting on his or her hands, awaiting the right person. They are the army of young men and women who are getting on with their lives, finding satisfying careers, buying what they need in life and having a bit left over for pleasure as well as saving and making plans for the future. They are the ones who are using both oars and making some headway against the tide.

But everyone is not like that. Some of the most angry, bitter, frustrated individuals I have ever met in my life are singles who had been convinced that "God has a plan for your life" and "a man for every plan!" It just didn't happen. Having felt the call of God to serve Him in missions, they responded, quite certain that in the process they would meet the right one and marry. As the tears vented the bitterness within, they expressed the feeling that God had let them down, that He had disappointed them.

Just a minute. God does have a plan for our lives. But does His promise to meet our needs necessarily come with a wedding ring attached to it? Or is this concept something which society has attached to our understanding of God's will? And when things don't measure up to our expectations, we feel hurt, abandoned, neglected and inadequate.

What Are the Chances?

A few years ago a study came out which indicated

that the older you are and the better educated you are as a female, the smaller chance you have of marriage. The study was alarming and disturbing. Bells and sirens went off. Notice of a nuclear disaster couldn't have been much more publicized. Later studies indicated that the pessimistic projections which alarmed so many were flawed.

What are the chances? Barbara Lovenheim says, "At age forty, a woman who has never been married has nearly a one in four chance of being married. A never-married man at forty has nearly a one in three chance of being married."[3]

So the answer is to get married earlier before the field gets picked over, right? Not necessarily. Early marriages don't guarantee either happiness or contentment. Being the right person is as important as marrying the right person. There is a definite correlation between your age and a sense of fulfillment and happiness in marriage—partly because as you grow older you have a much better idea of what kind of a person you want to marry—if you choose to do so—and you mature yourself. (A man who still puts his toy boats in his bathtub at age thirty still hasn't arrived!)

The answer to the question, "What are the chances?" isn't a statistic. It's either 100 percent or zero. Either God brings a person into your life who becomes your husband or wife or else God can give you the grace and strength to find contentment and fulfillment as a single.

Realizing that you may or may not marry, how do you look at your future?

The emergency procedure manual for a single-engine aircraft advises a pilot whose engine has failed to turn on the plane's landing lights when it gets to an altitude of 1,000 feet. Then, suggests the manual, when you get to 200 feet, if you don't like what you see, *turn them off again.*

That's what some do when it comes to the future. They live with rosy-eyed optimism or else a gloomy despair—"I just know I'll end up being an old maid (or a bachelor)!" But is turning off the lights or punching out the warning lights on the instrument panel of the plane the way to go?

What do you really want for your future?

__ Marriage
__ Fame
__ Money
__ Fulfillment
__ Happiness
__ Contentment
__ All of the above

Years ago, a single living in a couples' world reflected on his personal life and wrote, "I have learned the secret of being content in any and every situation, whether well fed or hungry, whether living in plenty or in want" (Philippians 4:12). He could have well added "whether single or married."

The reference from the New Testament probably helps you to identify the author: Paul, the man who penned thirteen of the New Testament letters. Very few people—either single or married—could say what Paul said.

Which of the following statements best describes your feelings as a single?

__ I'm content *all* of the time.
__ I'm content *most* of the time.
__ I'm content *some* of the time.
__ I'd lie if I said *any of the above.* Actually, I'm sick of being single and I'd like to be married. Anything would be an improvement over the way I feel right now.

Some folks are never content. Regardless of how beautiful the day, they will notice a cloud. No matter how great a job you do, they are the ones who pick out some slight flaw and bring it to your attention. They think they are perceptive when they are a pain in the neck.

Paul said that he had learned the secret of being content. Can we learn something from this man? Is our discontentment today—among both singles and married—the result of having missed something, something very important?

What were the circumstances of Paul's writing to the folks in the Roman city of Philippi? Was he writing from a beautiful condominium overlooking the Mediterranean? Was it from the swimming pool of the local Sheraton with a soft drink in his hand, dictating his thoughts to a beautiful girl by his side?

Hardly! Paul was under house arrest in Rome.

Though it is debatable as to whether he was actually in chains there as he was when he wrote to Timothy and Titus several years later, we *do* know he had lost his freedom—the ability to move about freely, to do whatever he wished whenever he wanted.

What produces contentment for most people today obviously wasn't a resource for Paul. I am fascinated by the biographies of great men and women. From them I have learned a great deal including the fact that most "great" men and women are just as completely human as those of us who never aspire to greatness, who live ordinary lives free from the celebrity status which we often think would be so wonderful. Paul had his ups and downs, but he had learned to cope with them in such a way that he was at peace with himself.

What Had Paul Learned Which Can Help Us Today?

There are steps to contentment in life which singles must work through if they are to come to grips with the future, no matter what it may hold. Think of them like mountain ranges with peaks and valleys through which you must pass before you reach the plain of contentment. I see five of them.

1. Believe in the goodness of God.

Several years ago a man who headed a growing, effective organization known as InterVarsity Christian Fellowship was killed in an automobile accident. He was in his prime! He was touching the lives of thousands if not millions. At the time his death was called tragic, a terrible accident. People wondered, "Why, God? Where were You to allow this to happen?" His name was Paul Little.

Shortly before his death, Little wrote a magazine article which contended that the bottom line of our theology is very simple: Is God good? Little contended that if God is essentially good, then whatever happens to us in life has been allowed by a loving Heavenly Father for a purpose which we may never fully understand but can accept.

When I read that article, I thought: "I'm not sure about this. It seems too simplistic to reduce all theology to a single premise." Then I began to think about what he wrote, evaluating many situations which defy explanation. I believe Little is right. Furthermore, every single living in a couples' world has to confront this very issue. *Is God a good God?* When you become convinced that He is both personal and good, then you learn to trust Him day by day. You resist the impulse to blame Him for what you consider to be undesirable in life, including your singleness.

2. *Believe that what happens to you is of concern to your Heavenly Father.*

Everything that I have learned about God came through the study of His Word, the Bible. When I studied philosophy, I learned something of what people think about life and our world, but the philosophers couldn't really tell me much about God Himself. When I studied science, I learned something of the awesome power which I see in our world. While science demonstrates something of the handiwork of the Almighty, it doesn't really tell me anything about God. Only the Bible does.

The apostle Paul says that when you became a believer in Jesus Christ, you were literally adopted into the family of God and became His child in a unique, special way. "Because you are sons," wrote Paul, "God sent the Spirit of his Son into our hearts, the Spirit who calls out, 'Abba, Father.' So you are no longer a slave, but a son; and since you are a son, God has made you also an heir" (Galatians 4:6-7).

The word that Paul used for "son" was a legal term which was applied to the concept of adoption under Roman law. It meant that the adopted individual had to be given the full rights of legal sonship. When he was adopted, in addition to taking the name of the adopting father, the person could never be held liable for crimes committed before the adoption. Furthermore, if other children were born to the adopting couple, the adopted individual could never be denied his inheritance.

That's a beautiful picture! Anyone who ponders what it means to be adopted by a loving couple today sees the parallels between this and our relationship to God.

"But I prayed about this, and God didn't hear my prayer!" Really! Have you ever considered the reality that God sometimes loves you too much to give you what you asked for? Just as your earthly father loved you enough to say, "No!" so our Father in heaven says the same thing.

Have you ever considered that what you thought of as a "lose-lose" situation was in reality the most "win-win" thing that could have happened to you? Think of all the messes that God may have kept you from when all of the time you thought He was indifferent to you and your situation. More than a few times I have prayed, "God, save me from myself. Your will is so much better than mine. Please, Father, no matter how strongly I want this, I want Your will even more."

And don't be like the young man who loved pastries (and he looked like it, too!), so he prayed, "Lord, if You want me to have that jelly-filled donut, please let me find a parking place right in front of the pastry shop." And you know what? He found it—on only the sixth trip around the block.

Much of the time God's working in our lives is subdued and quiet. You begin to see little patterns emerging. Then—bang!—things come together. You then look back and recognize the firm, loving hand of God in ways that you completely overlooked because your expectations of what you thought God should do were so different from what He believed you needed.

Question: What evidence do you have in your life that would remind you that God has been at work in your life? Think of the little things and remember that the big things in life are all the result of little things—the things which you may not have thought of as the result of God's care.

What happens to you is never a matter of indifference to God. In the Sermon on the Mount, Jesus said that the very hairs of your head are numbered (something which seems to require less and less effort on God's part in my case—see Luke 12:7). Accepting the implications of this means that what happens to me in my personal life—things which I consider to be both good and disappointing—must not be considered a matter of indifference to God; therefore, I must trust Him to meet the emotional and social needs of my life today and leave tomorrow in His hands.

3. Accept the circumstances as an indication of the will of God.

Paul often began his letters with a statement affirming that he was writing by the will of God. He also believed that the circumstances which seemed to be hostile to him were, nonetheless, subject to the control of the Father. "Yes," you say, "but is that necessarily true of my life today?"

The Bible says, "In him we were also chosen, having been predestined according to the plan of him who works out everything in conformity with the purpose of his will" (Ephesians 1:11). And though the promise brings hope and comfort to many singles (and frustrates some), it still stands there, towering like an oak that has endured many a storm: "And we know that in all things God works for the good of those who love him, who have been called according to his purpose" (Romans 8:28).

Either you believe that what God has told us in His Word is true, in spite of the fact you may not completely understand it, or else you have to come to the conclusion that you have been misled (i.e., God hasn't told you the truth).

So you don't like the situation you are in right now. What are your choices? The situation reminds me of the mountain climber who slipped and fell, ripping his ropes loose. On the way down, he grabbed an outcropping rock. He knew that even grasping this had to be nothing short of a miracle. Still trembling with fright, he looked down. He saw nothing below to which he could cling. He looked up, and there was nothing above which could help him get out of his dilemma. Suddenly, the climber heard a voice saying, "This is God calling. Turn loose; I'll catch you!" Again, looking below, he saw nothing. With hands perspiring, he yelled out, "Is there anybody *else* up there?"

Many of the options which singles are experimenting with today lead to greater disappointment and disillusionment. Regardless of the circumstances, you as a Christian single can hold to the assurance that you are God's child, and no matter how grim the circumstances of your life may appear to be right now, you can find comfort and peace in the assurance that God is still in control.

Jim Irwin, one of the *Apollo 15* astronauts, was a

personal friend of mine. Since his death, the friendship of this gracious, caring, patient man has become even more meaningful. Of all our conversations, I most value those that took place over a meal in a restaurant or just sitting and making small talk.

One afternoon Jim told about returning from the lunar rover vehicle (something like a very, very expensive golf cart) to the cabin of the landing module which would take them back to the spaceship. As Jim crawled into the cabin, he saw fragments of glass floating in the air. As he looked at the instrument panel and saw that the glass covering on one of the critical instruments had shattered, his heart sank and he broke out in a cold sweat. If the instrument itself had shattered, they were stranded! No way would they ever get back to the spacecraft.

Jim said that they vacuumed the floating fragments of glass, and to their great relief, when the instrument was activated, it worked perfectly. Only the glass—for whatever reason—had shattered.

Please forgive the analogy if you think it's corny, but hundreds and hundreds of singles write and tell me of shattered dreams and hopes which threaten to keep them from going where they want to be in life.

- "My girlfriend has an incurable cancer and I'm devastated!"

- "I think that I'm too good. When men find out I'm a virgin and intend to remain one until I marry, they lose interest in me fast."

- "I made the decision to date only those I would consider marrying. I sit at home and the phone never rings."

- "I don't know why God doesn't answer my prayer. My biological clock is running, and I haven't the faintest hope of marriage. What's wrong with me?"

Can you relate to some of that frustration?

The issue, of course, is not whether God is big enough or strong enough to meet your needs. Rather it is this: Is your faith strong enough to believe that He is still in control no matter what the temperature of your heart or the strength of the winds of adversity which blow?

A final thought before we go on. Weak faith in a *strong* plank is better than *strong* faith in a weak plank. And what does that mean? God is strong. You don't have to have great faith, only faith that He is in control of today, leaving tomorrow to His care and control. And how do you develop that conviction? First, go to the Book itself. It says that faith comes by hearing, and hearing by the Word (see Romans 10:17). Then listen to the testimonies of others who can say, "Look, I've been there. I found that God will keep His Word. You can trust Him."

4. *Understand that unpleasant circumstances are not forever.*

Part of Paul's secret was that he knew that being under house arrest wasn't forever, that there is more to life than what you see. In the AUTOEXEC.BAT of my computer I put a one-line reminder of this fact. It reads, "Remember, this too shall pass!" Some of the most frustrated singles that I have ever met are individuals who are unable to accept the fact that God is at work through even unpleasant circumstances.

As Malcolm Muggeridge put it, "Any happening, great and small . . . is a parable whereby God speaks to us; and the art of life is to get the message."

In the flyleaf of my Bible I penned the words of Andrew Murray, an Anglican minister of a century ago, who wrote:

> In times of trouble, God's trusting child may say: First: He brought me here; it is by His will I am in this straight [difficult] place: in that will I rest. Next: He will keep me here in His love, and give me grace in this trial to behave as His child. Then: He will make the trial a blessing, teaching me the lessons He intends me to learn, and working in me the grace He means to bestow. Last: In His good time He can bring me out again—how and when, He knows. Say: I

am here: 1. By God's appointment, 2. In His keeping, 3. Under His training, 4. For His time.

5. Wait patiently on God because He wills my best.

In chapter 7 I want to focus on how you can find God's will for the decisions of life, a task which is often misunderstood. Meanwhile, learning to live one day at a time, finding His strength to do what needs to be done today is all part of the lesson which ultimately brings understanding.

Paul's secret can be yours. The American humorist Mark Twain used to say that we are all about as happy as we decide to be. I think Paul would have agreed.

Endnotes

1. R.C. Sproul, *Lifeviews: Understanding the Ideas That Shape Society Today* (Old Tappan, NJ: Revell, 1980), p. 137.

2. George Barna, "Marriage and Divorce Toward the Year 2000," *Single Adult Ministries Journal* (Colorado Springs, CO: January, 1990), p. 3.

3. Barbara Lovenheim, *Beating the Marriage Odds: When You Are Smart, Single and over 35* as quoted by Ray Mossholder in *Singles Plus* (Lake Mary, FL: Creation House, 1991), p. 38.

2

Winning over Your Biggest Enemies

*"We have met the enemy
and he is us!"*

—*Pogo*

*D*o singles have more in common than marrieds? "No!" says researcher George Barna. He contends that singles cannot be lumped into one category since those who are single today come from at least three subgroups: the never-been-marrieds; the formerly marrieds; and the widowed. Even so, I suspect that even among the "never-been-marrieds" there are several subsubgroups such as the "never-been-married-but-want-to-fast," the "never-been-married-and-not-in-a-hurry-to-get-hitched" group and the "no-way-am-I-going-to-give-up-my-fun" group!

On a more serious note, Barna also believes that there is less theological consensus among singles who consider themselves to be Christians than among their married counterparts. Older singles tend to take the Bible more at face value; younger ones tend to think that what the Bible says about their lives isn't binding, especially when their lifestyle is in pretty flagrant contradiction of what God says about the way we should live.

Younger singles—say those under age thirty-five—tend to believe that the Ten Commandments are "not relevant" and the idea of sin is "outdated." A far greater percentage who are themselves products of unhappy or dysfunctional homes believe that prayer doesn't change circumstances. Singles often confess to feelings of helplessness, especially women who are not very prone to initiate friendships with members of the opposite sex. But feeling helpless as a single in a couples' world is a lot different than feeling hopeless.

You may be expecting me to come up with a Bible verse and use it like a Band-Aid, saying, "See—here's the answer to this whole problem!" The situation is more complex than that.

There are at least five issues which you have to work through as a single which I consider to be enemies of your peace of mind and contentment. In almost every publication on singles, no matter how they may differ, you will discover that there is universal agreement over the fact that the greatest problem confronting singles today is *loneliness.* So consider this the number one issue, right? Wrong. I put it second on my list to your number one problem—yourself.

Singles' Enemy #1: Yourself

One of my favorite cartoons focuses on a little character by the name of Pogo who, with his friends, is going out to do battle with the "enemy." The first few frames of the cartoon show Pogo and company with their swords and spears ready to do mortal combat. Then, the same group is shown coming back from the battle dragging their spears and swords in the dust. Underneath is the caption, "We have met the enemy, and he is us!" That's powerful.

This entire book is about helping you come to grips with the reality of your life, and after realistically assessing where you are, formulate a game plan that will let you get your life moving forward.

Some of you have grown up with difficult situations. Some of you have been abused by parents and perhaps by people you once considered to be your friends.

None of us can control the circumstances which confront us, but we can control how we respond to them. When you find yourself in situations which you don't like, which of the following statements or phrases best describes your negative reactions?

___ Retreat into yourself.
___ Deny what is happening.
___ Refuse to talk about the situation.
___ Run—move to a new home or quit your job.
___ Withdraw from the circle of friends or acquaintances.
___ Struggle with a sense of failure, thinking something is wrong with you.
___ Feel guilty.
___ Transfer your anger to someone else and take out your frustration on another.
___ Keep up a front—smile but cry inside.
___ Tell everyone who will listen how you have been mistreated.
___ Get so busy that you don't have time to think about it.
___ Plan for sweet revenge.
___ Cling to the hope that things will change.

__ Refuse to be with couples or families because you feel like a misfit.

__ Exaggerate or boast about social contacts or exploits.

While you may be your own worst enemy, you are also the solution to your needs. Understanding who you are—that you are a person uniquely created in the image of God, that of all the other 6 billion people in the world there is not another just like you—is all part of the armor that keeps the situations of life, including the wounds of well-meaning but harmful friends, from crippling you.

To belittle yourself, deprecate your value and deny needs which may exist in your life doesn't lessen your true worth. This is neither a matter of pride nor arrogance, but simply an understanding of how God views your life. No one sees through your eyes. No one feels what you feel. No one understands and senses what you do.

It is tremendously important to realize that you are a whole person *now* (period!). Thinking that marriage will complete you only underlines the insecurity which you have—something which needs to be dealt with. When you become a believer, God's Holy Spirit comes to take up residence in your life, filling you with His presence and enabling you to be all that He intends. How does He make a difference, though, in coping with that greatest single need—the need for companionship?

Singleness forces you to make decisions and choices which you may not want to make, especially if you are a woman. Shall I embark on a career as opposed to getting married and having children? Will I need to think about buying a home or getting my own apartment? Do I need to get serious about saving some money for the future?

Says Carolyn Koons and Michael Anthony in *Single Adult Passages:*

> When a never-married or newly single woman faces her future, she is forced to make decisions about matters traditionally considered in the male domain. She must choose among educational and career options, allocate her financial resources according to housing, transportation, and other material needs, and make a host of other decisions that depend on sound judgment and conviction.[1]

People who don't want to face those issues remind me of the ill-fated crew of a U.S. Air Force bomber of World War II vintage.

Here's what happened. Some thirty years after the plane went down in the Sahara it was discovered. At first, the men who saw it thought it was a mirage. They could not believe their eyes. It was an airplane, almost intact, sitting on the sands of a vast desert. They knew it was not a new plane because it had bomb turrets and two big propeller-driven engines. Sure enough—it was a U.S. Air Force bomber, preserved by the hot, dry air for three decades. On the side of the fuselage, still visible, were the words *"Lady Be Good."*

And when *Lady Be Good* was found, one of the unsolved mysteries of the war was also solved. You see, *Lady Be Good* along with her crew took off for a mission in North Africa and was never heard from again. But when the plane was found, a second mystery was unearthed. How did the plane get to be 400 miles beyond its destination? When aeronautic specialists inspected the aircraft, they found that the instruments on the plane were still working—some thirty years later—and still accurate. Investigators came to the conclusion that the plane had overshot its destination by some 400 miles because it got into a high altitude air current that doubled its speed without the crew even knowing it.

What evidently happened was that the crew knew how long the flight ordinarily took, and when they reached their destination in half the time, they did not believe their instruments and kept flying. Eventually they ran out of fuel and the plane drifted down into the desert sand 400 miles beyond their destination. Searchers found the remains of the crew 100 miles across the sand from the plane. The story of *Lady Be Good,* the plane whose crew would not believe its instruments, is a parable about those who refuse to believe the instrument panel of life and adjust accordingly. On the practical side of this illustration, ask yourself:

- How old am I?

- Have I avoided making decisions about the future thinking that someone would come along and I would marry?

- What am I waiting on before I decide to move ahead?

Remember, there are some things which God or your mother won't do for you. You've got to do them on your own, and when you fail to face the circumstances of your life and come up with a game plan, you have made the decision to fail. Tough as it is in facing that issue, it's wise to acknowledge the realities of life and move ahead. You'll be much happier in the long run.

Singles' Enemy #2: Loneliness

In the Garden God said, "It is not good for the man to be alone. I will make a helper suitable for him" (Genesis 2:18). Things haven't changed much. We came from the drawing board of heaven designed for companionship, and when—for whatever reason—it is denied, loneliness, like a fog which obscures and separates us from the reality of our surroundings, begins to move in.

Let me tell you about a senior single, Mrs. Jean Rosenstein, and what happened to her. Mrs. Rosenstein sat down at a small table in her cramped, one-bedroom apartment and painfully put her thoughts about loneliness on paper. The arthritis in her fingers made the writing difficult and painful.

The scrawled words read,

> I'm so lonely I could die. So alone, I cannot write. My hands and fingers pain me. . . . I see no human beings. My phone never rings. I'm so very old and so very lonely. I hear from no one. I am way past eighty years. Should I die? Never had any kind of holidays, no kind. My birthday is this month. I even feel sure the world ended, I'm the only one on earth. How else can I feel: All alone. See no one. . . . Hear no one. Oh, dear God, help me!!! Am I of sound mind, so lonely very, very much. I do not know what to do.

She put the letter in an oversized yellow envelope along with some money and six stamps and mailed it to a newspaper. The money was to pay for the call if someone would call just to talk to her. The stamps were for anyone who would write.

In a city of almost 8 million people, Jean Rosenstein felt very much alone. And what happened? First, a reporter called and said that he would like to come. Mrs. Rosenstein was delighted. The reporter found that her letter was accurate, painfully accurate. She told the reporter, "If you are alone, you die every day. . . . Sometimes I just dread to see myself wake up in the morning." The reporter published her letter, along with the description I have shared with you. And then what happened?

In the next two weeks following the story, thousands of letters and cards poured into the little apartment. Visitors streamed in and out to talk to the lonely little lady who had no friends. So many people called that the telephone had to be taken from the hook. Letters came from elderly people, young couples with pictures of their children, boys and girls, people from all over the world. As eighty-four-year-old Jean Rosenstein sat amidst the sacks of mail, she said, "This will last for the rest of my life."

Probably you, like myself, say three cheers for everybody who responded to Mrs. Rosenstein. But there are thousands of Mrs. Rosensteins around the world, and, believe me, they are not all elderly. They are Filipina nurses working in hospitals in the United States, trying to make enough money to send some home to help a hurting family. They are single workers in Saudi, Korea, Singapore and elsewhere estranged from the comfortable surroundings of home. They are the multitude of singles who feel cut off from the mainstream of life and society, neglected by those too busy to care. They are the ones who feel they are losing their sanity in a couples' world.

The composer Peter Tchaikovsky knew what loneliness was. He raised the shades of the window of his heart as he wrote in a minor key, "None but the lonely heart can feel my anguish. . . ."

Mother Theresa called loneliness "the hunger for human love," and described it as "the world's worst ill."

"It is the most desolate word in all human language," says Chuck Swindoll. "It is capable of hurling the heaviest weights the heart can endure. It plays no favorites, ignores all rules of courtesy, knows neither border nor barrier, yields no mercy, refuses all bargains, and holds the clock in utter contempt."[2] It is loneliness, one of the most terrible maladies to strike our existence.

One of the strangest things about the malady is that you can be in the midst of people and yet loneliness strikes. An American expatriot pressed his face to the windowpane as he watched people hurrying toward the warmth of their homes and turned away to write the words, "Be it ever so humble, there's no place like home."

Ask the man or woman whose hospital room has made existence like that of a prisoner, or the elderly woman who lives by herself, who goes to the store daily and spends but a few coins just to see someone else. Telephone operators report that there are certain individuals who have made it a practice to call at about the same time every day, usually on the pretext of needing a number, when actually they just want to hear the warmth of a human voice.

Ask Al Sanders, a well-known media personality, about loneliness. He'll tell you about the time he misdialed the telephone while trying to make a local call. As soon as he heard an elderly voice on the telephone, he realized that he had dialed the wrong number, apologized and prepared to disconnect, when the voice said, "No, wait! I am eighty years old, and no one ever calls me. Would you talk to me for a minute?"

Ask the celebrity who is surrounded with fans seeking autographs, and you may be surprised to learn that some of the world's most influential and well-known people are also some of its loneliest people.

Take, for example, actress Doris Day, once voted the world's most popular actress, who candidly confessed that she was an extremely lonely woman and often cried herself to sleep. Speaking of the emptiness in her life she asked, "If so many people love me, how come I'm alone?" The musician Sting described himself as "the spokesman for loneliness and alienation."

It is not only the extremely talented along with the sick, the imprisoned and the elderly who are lonely. Ask the single parent who puts the kids to bed and dares not to turn off the radio or television. Ask the businessman who is burned out and fearful of letting his boss know he needs help. Ask the teenage girl who is pregnant and dreads telling her parents. These are experts in loneliness. They know because they hurt.

There are two things of which you can be sure: God knows the anguish of your loneliness and hurt, and He cares. He cares infinitely more deeply than you can comprehend. Do you remember the loneliness that Jesus Christ faced as the disciples turned one by one and left Him? Remember His pain as He cried out, "My God, my God, why have you forsaken me?" (Mark 15:34). Do you recall the long hours prior to the ordeal at Calvary when He struggled in prayer in the garden and wrestled with the anguish which was before Him?

Do you remember how Jesus prayed, "My Father, if it is possible, may this cup be taken from me" (Matthew 26:39)? Was He afraid of dying? Afraid of the nails which would be driven through His hands and feet? No! What He was asking was that He not be separated from the presence of the Father. In other words He was praying *that He might be spared the loneliness of separation from the Father's presence.*

Jesus is a specialist when it comes to the pain of loneliness, and that's part of the reason that He provides a remedy for your hurt. Because He suffered the pain of loneliness as He was separated from the Father, you need never be separated from His presence. It's the difference between being alone and being lonely.

Why so much loneliness today?

There are some reasons. The backdrop for much of our loneliness today actually began two or three generations ago with the move to the big cities, because that's where the work was. Behind the barren walls and the locked doors, the beauty of the countryside was forgotten. The asphalt streets and the polluted air have caused us to lose touch with the freshness of the dew on the grass in the early morning and the crispness of a new dawn. We have forgotten what the horizon looks like at sunset, as the blazing sun paints the western sky myriad shades of red and orange—colors never captured by an artist's palette.

We tell ourselves that this is all the price of progress, that a job, or a better job overseas, justifies all of this. But far more than *where* we live, it is the *how we live* that produces loneliness.

Much of our loneliness is the result of feeling unaccepted—in a family, on the job or among friends. The result? We withdraw and hide. Dr. James Lynch, a psychologist, says:

> There is an almost unconscious cultural conspiracy to fool people into thinking that to be alone is a virtue. The myth of independence, which one sees every day in advertising and other media, makes it appear that to admit we need each other is a sign of weakness.[3]

What's the cure for the problem?

Is there a cure for loneliness? Mother Theresa said there is. Remember that she described loneliness as the world's "worst ill"? But she contended the answer is love and involvement in the lives of other people. She believed that in reaching out to help a hurting person, you find a cure for that demon of loneliness.[4]

Some of the work in our own office at *Guidelines* is done by volunteers who thank us for the privilege of being part of the group (when in reality it is we who are indebted to them). The alternative to loneliness for some singles is to get out and to use their talents and time for the Lord. Your church may provide the resource you need to combat loneliness. I don't think I have ever seen a church or a Christian organization which had so many people volunteer to work with kids, to stuff envelopes or help in various programs that it couldn't use a few more. Why not try the cure?

Contact with people often leads to friendships which is part of the answer to loneliness. That's why I have devoted a chapter to developing non-sexual friendships. Sometimes, driven by loneliness, we reach out to others which may result in friendships that will last forever. That was the way it was with Joseph Scrivens, whose lovely fiancée was drowned in a Canadian lake. Feeling lost and lonely, he found the friendship of Jesus Christ, a Person who drives away the loneliness of separation. It was of this unending friendship that Joseph Scrivens wrote when he penned these words, "What a friend we have in Jesus, all our sins and griefs to bear! What a privilege to carry everything to God in prayer. Oh, what peace we often forfeit, oh, what needless pain we bear, all because we do not carry everything to God in prayer!"

Fighting loneliness? A theater critic recently closed his column saying, "If you're feeling blue and lonely, stop by and see a movie. It probably won't cheer you up, but at least you can feel sorry for someone else." There's a better way—the way of love as you help someone else who hurts. Unlock the door of your life, take a lingering look at the beauty which God has placed around you and go find someone else who is lonely and needs a friend.

We need each other, and we need the friendship of One who will never leave or forsake us.

Singles' Enemy #3: Sexual frustration

> Dear Sir,
> I caught part of your message on CBN [Christian Broadcasting Network] concerning sex and marriage. I am a Christian and single. I have many friends, precious friends. My problem—I've always thought sex without marriage was wrong and have never gone that route, but I still have those desires and it is getting harder and harder to hold on to those principles. I still cannot bring myself to indulge in sex out of marriage. What are we single people to do? I've prayed that God would send someone, a husband, Christian husband who would be right for me and I for him. What can I do? I cannot bring myself to talk to my pastor concerning this problem.

Coping with sexual frustration is never easy!

"Christians often assume that because they are followers of Jesus they shouldn't have any major problems with sex," says Ronald Burwell.[5] But such is not the case. We live in a sex-saturated environment. Television, the movies, the suggestiveness of talk shows on radio and television and the openness with which society has embraced sex constantly serves as a reminder to singles of what his or her hormones say almost every day, "You are a sexual being."

At the same time our contemporary culture expects you to be sexually active. The single who is celibate is often considered a Victorian throwback, someone who is indeed quaint in the free-wheeling world of today. The vast majority of high school students know more about sex and certainly have had more sexual experience than did college graduates a generation ago. National surveys also indicate that religious faith has very little to do with abstinence when it comes to sexual activity. Fear of AIDS seems to be a greater deterrent to an active sex life that the fear of God.

In answer to the question, "How do I handle the issue of sexual activity?" there are three alternatives:

1. As an antidote to loneliness and sexual frustration, do what most singles do: Protect yourself to the extent that you can, use discretion, but go ahead and "do it."

Without writing a "book" in rebuttal of this premise, may I simply say that *it just doesn't work.* Throwing yourself into a relationship to relieve boredom or escape loneliness leaves you frustrated, empty within, feeling abandoned, cheapened and guilty if you have any sense of conscience.

Question: Does God say no sex before marriage to take the fun out of life? Besides, everybody is doing it.

Let's take the last part first. You have a valid point when you say that sexual activity among mature singles is common. A host of statistics can be summoned to back up that view.

In the '60s and '70s the sexual revolution changed a lot of things, including society's acceptance of sexual activity outside of marriage. The pill generally eliminated the concern about pregnancy, and the availability of abortions served as a backup for unwanted pregnancies. The playboy attitude of "It's OK as long as you love somebody and you both agree" became the practice of society and, in spite of what the church officially says, also became the practice of many singles who consider themselves to be Christians. Then, as the effect of this began to take its toll, the number of individuals—especially women—who had been wounded began to make it clear that lacking the commitment of marriage, sexual relations cannot meet the psychological needs of men and women.

God's point of view is very clear:

> It is God's will that you should be sanctified: that you should avoid sexual immorality; that each of you should

learn to control his own body in a way that is holy and honorable, not in passionate lust like the heathen, who do not know God; and that in this matter no one should wrong his brother or take advantage of him. The Lord will punish men for all such sins, as we have already told you and warned you. (1 Thessalonians 4:3-6)

Is it possible that rather than striving to take the "fun" out of life, God knew what was necessary for humankind to find fulfillment and happiness? Sexual activity outside of marriage just doesn't fit into the formula of fulfillment and happiness which God intends for us.

2. *The second alternative, simply put, is to repress your sexuality.*

Studies which the Vatican has not circulated very widely indicate that those who practice the monastic life, those who should know what sexual repression is about, are not very successful in doing it. Priests and nuns confess that they may be trying to focus on spiritual things, but their minds fantasize sexual experiences which would embarrass them greatly to share. Because sexual repression is difficult at best, especially for males, who are aroused visually, Paul instructed, "Now to the unmarried and the widows I say: It is good for them to stay unmarried, as I am. But if they cannot control themselves, they should marry, for it is better to marry than to burn with passion" (1

Corinthians 7:8-9). The term which Paul used for passion makes it clear that he is talking about sexual passion.

Some consider Paul's words to be rather strange. Why say that it is good to remain single as he was? A valid question such as that needs to be addressed. Paul had no ax to grind with marriage. To the contrary, he recognized it as a beautiful God-given relationship which was so designed to allow for free and open sexual expression. However, the persecution which came to a boil under Nero had already begun as Paul was writing, and he was saying that marriage brought with it the risk of having a relationship torn through imprisonment and, perhaps, even by the death of one or both. But even so, he recognized the explosive power of our sexuality and says that marriage is the solution to the sexual pressures of singleness. Repressing or denying your sexuality is about as sensible as denying that you have ears or feet. There has to be a better way.

3. The answer: Coping with sexual frustration.

As a single you can't avoid the reality of our world—the beach; the visual depiction of sex on television and at the theater which leaves little to the imagination; fashion, even the scintillating ads for women's underwear in magazines and newspapers; the soap operas on TV and what have you. Sexual passion is like a fire which either is contained in the boiler or is fed. The more you focus on sex, the more miserable you will become. Daydreaming, fantasies, pornography, sexually orientated movies and videos all feed the dragon of lust.

When you struggle with visual images which inflame your passions, taking cold showers or running for ten kilometers may help, but that's not enough. There has to be more.

Go public with your commitment. Those of us who are uncertain of where we stand are much more prone to be swayed by emotion than by a knowledge of right or wrong. We begin to reason that God made us as sexual beings and put this furnace of passion with our bodies, and so surely to bring to fulfillment what He designed can't be wrong. Or can it?

When our daughters were dating and suitors began to become more than "just friends," our girls made it plain that they were perfectly normal and that they appreciated the attention, but they were virgins and intended to remain that way until they were married. Anybody who really loves a girl will respect that kind of commitment, and anyone who does not is not the kind of an individual that should be considered as a possible mate.

I would also like to point out that in spite of the openness of sex today, there is a growing army of men and women—usually ignored by the press—who have made the commitment to wait until marriage.

Be willing to be accountable. If you are serious about sexual purity, then be willing to be accountable to a small group of individuals you respect who will keep confidence with you, people who are willing to ask the tough questions. Meet with each other on a regular basis and be willing to be open and vulnerable with each other, honestly confessing your needs. I suggest that each make a threefold commitment:

1. Keep confidence with each other, not discussing details outside the group. Honest confession can be dangerous. "Christians don't gossip," chides my daughter. "They just share prayer requests."

2. Make a commitment to encourage and help each other.

3. Pray for each other.

Make a vow of celibacy and/or sexual purity before God. This is strong medicine, and I would not recommend it at all unless you have a made a serious commitment to the Lord and have enough of the fear of the Almighty in you that once you have made your vow, you will have no hesitation in keeping it completely. The Bible says, "When you make a vow to God, do not delay in fulfilling it. He has no pleasure in fools; fulfill your vow. It is better not to vow than to make a vow and not fulfill it" (Ecclesiastes 5:4-5).

When couples become convicted that they are going beyond the point of discretion in a relationship, by mutual consent they may vow before the Lord to withhold further sexual expression until they are married. In that case, should one weaken, the other should remind him or her that vows to the Lord are serious and not to be taken lightly.

A word of warning. If you feel that you lack the strength to follow through on a vow, don't make it. But with the vow comes a strengthening that helps your resolve.

Don't feed the fire. God's not going to throw the switch for you, turning off your sexual desires and then flip it back on when you marry. That's why you have to exercise resolve when it comes to sexual stimulation. If you sit and watch a sexually explicit video or movie, of course your emotions will be affected. You're normal. God doesn't replace your hormones with ice water because you are a Christian.

This also means that you will have to decide how far you can go in a relationship and maintain your sexual purity. Some couples excuse sexual intimacies by saying, "We didn't have sex!" But they did everything short of it.

Sexual purity isn't a matter of what you can do or not do. It is a matter of the heart, respecting each other's bodies and waiting until you have become one through marriage. Then what is so wrong before you are married becomes so right. It's all a matter of timing. As Ray Mossholder put it, "God doesn't say no to sex outside marriage because He's trying to be a spoilsport or prude. He says no so that you'll enjoy maximum sex once you're married. To accept less than that is to accept less than God's best for you."[6]

Yield your mind and body to the Lord. Prior to

the 1964 rebellion in the Congo, Dr. Helen
Roseveare served as a missionary. When she returned home to her native land, she desperately
sought for a marriage partner. She says:

> For years I had counseled girls that "the
> fellow who fools with you is not the man
> who marries you." I knew all the rules,
> but I didn't obey them when it came to
> my own desperate need. By the time I re-
> gained my senses, I had created an awful
> mess. I felt I had lost everything. I didn't
> lose my faith, but I lost my relationship
> with the Father and all sense of peace.[7]

Some would have told her, "Your standard is too
high. Come on, be realistic. You are a sexual person and because God made you that way, you
can't be that wrong!" Confused and feeling guilty,
Helen resigned from the mission and spent a miserable two years wondering what to do with her
life. Finally, realizing that she needed to go back,
she was recommissioned to missionary service.
She went through the motions, saying the right
things and doing the right things. But she was
miserable. Like David of old, her heart yearned for
restored fellowship with the Father but it just
didn't come.

Then during the Congo rebellion, rebel soldiers
invaded the compound where she was serving.
She was taken by the rebels and savagely raped.
Eventually she recovered, but the rape triggered

sexual impulses which had to be confronted. And
how did God meet her? She explained:

> Strangely enough, rape, though cruel,
> woke me up. Having no previous sexual
> experiences, I suddenly found I was a
> woman. All my passions were aroused,
> and I hadn't a clue to what to do with
> them. It seems terrible that such wicked-
> ness could cause this. But it did.
>
> "I can satisfy you," God said.
>
> "You don't know what you're talking
> about," I argued. "I don't need an elusive
> spiritual husband. I want a man with arms."
>
> But God kept reminding me, "I will
> supply all your need." In absolute de-
> spair I cried out, "Okay, God. If You re-
> ally mean it, it's up to You."
>
> Right then, at every level of my need,
> God met me. I didn't have a clue to my
> inner hungers—and I didn't think God
> did either. But He did know. He meant it
> when He said He would be to me a hus-
> band (Isaiah 54:5). He quieted my de-
> sires and gave sweet, refreshing sleep. I
> awoke with a new awareness of the love
> of God, and a new understanding that I
> was accepted of Him.
>
> Not only did the Lord bring satisfac-
> tion and release, but He also brought a
> new lightness of heart and a new joy.[8]

When Christ is Master and Lord, He is also able to help you subdue the dragon. One of the passages which has helped me personally is Second Corinthians 10:4-5, where Paul wrote:

> The weapons we fight with are not the weapons of the world. On the contrary, they have divine power to demolish strongholds. We demolish arguments and every pretension that sets itself up against the knowledge of God, and we take captive every thought to make it obedient to Christ.

Martin Luther contended that you can't keep the birds from flying overhead, but you can keep them from building a nest in your hair. How does that translate? The sight of a pretty girl with a nice figure or a good-looking male who is well muscled may well cause your heart to skip a beat. We are made in such a way that there is an attraction to the opposite sex. You can't help that, but from that point on you are responsible for what you do. When you mentally undress the girl or imagine what his body pressed against yours would feel like, God holds you responsible for your thoughts.

When you catch yourself thinking what you know is lustful and wrong, quickly confess it, and ask for God's help to bring those thoughts into captivity to the obedience of Jesus Christ.

Fantasy and "make-believe sex" should never be

part of the life of one who has submitted his or her life and future to the Savior. Remember He said, "You have heard that it was said, 'Do not commit adultery.' But I tell you that anyone who looks at a woman lustfully has already committed adultery with her in his heart" (Matthew 5:27-28). Until God brings a marriage partner into your life who can satisfy your sexual urges, provided that is His will, God can give you the grace to cope with those biological desires.

In the meanwhile yield this part of your life to the control of the Holy Spirit. In his book *The Great Divorce*, C.S. Lewis told of a group of people who were given a second chance to go to heaven provided they gave up the sin which had blocked their entrance to heaven. One in the group, a young man, had a lizard on his shoulder which symbolized his sexual hang-ups. The messenger asks the young man to give up the burden, saying, "Just let me take that lizard off your shoulder." The youth hesitates as the lizard whispers, "You know that he will take all your fun away if you let him kill me." He is torn. He wants to yield to what he believes is right yet is fearful at the same time. Finally he gives up the lizard, crying out in anguish. But then, suddenly, a transformation takes place. The lizard becomes a radiant golden stallion. Ronald Burwell explains, "The tawdry, second-rate sexuality represented by the lizard is transformed into the proper, powerful, majestic sexuality that God planned for us."[9]

The resources of His help make the difference

which allows you to keep your sanity and your moral purity as a single in a couples' world.

Singles' Enemy #4: Financial problems

In their teen years singles are visionaries and dreamers. At the very time when their sexual libido is at its highest, their ability to process realism is at its very lowest. Maturity doesn't come overnight. It is a slow process, often brought about by trial and error.

In their twenties singles have a great deal of freedom. Most no longer are under the supervision of parents. College life yields to a steady job with an income. Most singles gradually cease to rely on support from their parents and move toward economic independence. When you are single and not supporting a family, your buying power is greatly enhanced. Cars, clothes, entertainment, travel, music systems, computers and things which were previously beyond your reach financially are now available.

For most singles who are twentysomething, the economic realities of life have not fully set in. After all, you reason, there's plenty of time to settle down and think about economic independence in the future. But toward the end of this decade, the reality hits home for those who are still single. *Hey,* you begin to think, *I'm not getting any younger. I suppose I should really start thinking about my future.*

By age thirty most men have settled on a career choice, and by then most women are either expecting a knight in shining armor to come swooping down for them very quickly, or, like it or not, they have to start doing some serious economic planning.

Interested in using money wisely? Without a lot of comment, I would like to give you ten guidelines that can make a tremendous difference in your reaching economic independence.

Guideline #1: Make God—not money—your goal in life and reason for existing.

You tell me what you are living for, and I'll tell you whom you really serve. George MacDonald, the man who greatly influenced C.S. Lewis, wrote, "It is not the rich man only who is under the dominion of things; they, too, are slaves who having no money are unhappy from it." Those who live simply for things usually have pretty shallow lives. Seek first God's kingdom and you will be amazed how He blesses you with the things which money cannot buy.

Guideline #2: Live within your income.

And don't be like the young woman who said, "I am committed to living within my income even if I have to borrow money to do it." You may be thinking, "This guy Sala is really out of touch with reality." If I am, successful business people are also wrong. Today the scourge of consumer credit (How many credit card offers did you receive when you got into college?) is dragging some singles to the pits of economic chaos. Credit comes easy. Why wait? Get it now and enjoy it.

Dr. Edward Kantzian, associate professor of psychiatry at Harvard Medical School, says, "For people to admit they can't afford things they want means placing themselves in a position of weakness. They have to say no to themselves and nobody wants to do that."

Saying no to debt means saying yes to your future. Besides being practical, this concept is biblical. "Let no debt remain outstanding," writes Paul, "except the continuing debt to love one another" (Romans 13:8).

Live within your income by budgeting your money, realizing money is a trust, not a means of indulgence or a weapon. Never spend money you do not have to impress people you do not like, buying things you do not need. Otherwise, you end up hurting yourself.

Guideline #3: Resist impulse buying.

Because some singles have more discretionary money (that means money that you can spend for whatever you like) than their married counterpart, they become targets of the merchants who prey on emotions. Before you buy something which you like but don't need and didn't intend to buy when you went shopping, ask three questions:

1. Do I need it?
2. Do I have a place to put it?
3. Can I afford it?

If you don't come up with yes answers to all three questions, think twice before you say, "Yes, I'll take that!"

Guideline #4: Avoid nonappreciating purchases for which you must pay interest.

One of the greatest threats to your economic independence is credit card buying. There's nothing easy about "easy payments." You increase your buying power by at least forty percent when you avoid paying interest which ranges from eighteen to forty percent per year.

Guideline #5: Borrow money only for items that will appreciate in value.

Like what? Few items fall into this category. Over a long period of time, real estate generally appreciates, but most of the things which you want to borrow money to enjoy, such as vacations, trips, TVs, clothes, CD players and so forth, do not fall into this category.

What about borrowing money for a car? Having a car is usually an economic necessity to provide transportation. But the kind that you buy determines whether it is a necessary investment which allows you to hold down a job, thus creating income, or a luxury with bells and whistles you don't need. Be on guard against the line the car salesman gives you. Get some advice and buy what you need but no more. The bells and whistles can wait.

Guideline #6: Save friendships by saying, "Sorry, but I can't do it" when your friends want to borrow money from you.

The Bible says that the borrower becomes a servant to the lender. More friendships—good ones, too—are hurt by borrowing money than by anything else (excluding borrowing boyfriends or girlfriends).

John was best friends with Meri—not romantically involved but moving that direction. The payment was two months late on his car and he was concerned about the finance company's picking it up. "I'll loan you the money if you can pay me back by the first of the month when my rent is due," said Meri as they had a soda together.

John borrowed the money, and then got laid off the next weekend when the construction job he was working finished early. When the first of the month came and John didn't call, Meri called him. "I'll have it in a week," John told her without the faintest notion of where the money was coming from.

When he didn't have the money, Meri had to borrow it from her parents. From that point on their relationship was strained. Meri felt that John couldn't be trusted.

Guideline #7: Make good investments but avoid get-rich-quick schemes.

That phrase "old so soon and smart so late" is never more true than when it comes to the economic realities of single life. Take, for example, the power of compound interest.

Let say that you are age twenty-one, and upon graduation from college, your father gives you $100. Thereafter, you put away the same amount every month in an investment which will average ten percent per year. By age sixty-five that practice would have resulted in a nest egg of $963,647.25—enough to live comfortably for the rest of your life.

On the other hand, let's say that you wait until age forty and put away the same amount of money each month at the same amount of interest. Your savings would amount to only $134,994.75. There's a tremendous difference.

A word of warning from the experience of one who has been there himself: Sooner or later you are going to have a friend come to you and say, "Look, I like you. You're my friend so I'm going to let you in on a great deal which will give you a 300 percent return on your investment, but you've gotta go on this right now." Beware! Greed is the enemy of safe investments. There's no free lunch, and anything that good is suspect.

Guideline #8: Demonstrate that what you have belongs to the Lord by following the Bible's teaching on giving.

Just a minute, you may be thinking. *Why should I give anything to God? This is* my *money. I earned it.* The practice of tithing, or giving a tenth of your income back to the Lord, may be something totally new to you. But the practice isn't new. It goes clear back to the days of Abraham, Isaac and Jacob in the Old Testament.

"Do I have to do this to please God?"

"No," I would answer, but I am convinced that those who practice this see blessings and a return on their investment in ways that cannot be assessed in just terms of monetary gain. Strange as the mathematics appear, God takes the nine-tenths remaining and makes it go further than the whole would go. How do I know? I began this practice as a single, continued it in our marriage and have seen God honor the promises of His word in this regard for years. (For additional biblical references see 1 Corinthians 16:2, Luke 6:38 and Malachi 3:10.)

Guideline #9: Remember the less fortunate than yourself.

Proverbs 19:17 says, "He who is kind to the poor lends to the LORD, and he will reward him for what he has done."

Guideline #10: Lay up treasure in heaven.

Jesus put it like this:

> Do not store up for yourselves treasures on earth, where moth and rust destroy, and where thieves break in and steal. But store up for yourselves treasures in heaven, where moth and rust do not destroy, and where thieves do not break in and steal. For where your treasure is, there your heart will be also. (Matthew 6:19-21)

This means you begin to develop a life purpose. OK, trying finishing this statement in a few sentences: "What I am living for is _____.

Now, let's go on to that fifth enemy of singles.

Singles' Enemy #5:
Meaningless relationships

The choice of singles to be sexually active has much less to do with lust than it does the desire to establish a good relationship. Our need for people is so great that we are often driven by it to accept situations which we know are not in our best interest.

Item #1: Rhonda grew up in a dysfunctional home. Her father escaped from prison, met her mother and got her pregnant. She never really had a relationship with the man who lived with her mother until she was about two years of age.

Thereafter, as she was growing up, a succession of men lived with her mother, none of whom was really a dad to her. She did know, however, the rejection and even the abuse that comes by living in such an environment. At the age of sixteen, she ran away from home, choosing to live with a boyfriend who also gave her a child before going his way. "What I was really looking for," she explained, "was not sex but someone to love me."

Item #2: "I thought that marriage would be the solution to my financial problems," one young woman whom I'll call Pat confided in me. It was the solution *temporarily*, but married to a man fourteen years her senior, Pat soon lost interest. He wanted to spend his Saturdays watching television; she wanted to go places and do things. She eventually did—without him, and in the process she met someone that she felt better met her needs and left her husband.

Item #3: "But I'm all alone. Living with someone would surely be better than being lonely." One of the problems of immature thinking is that you become so influenced by "need," that you become blinded to the realities of the consequences of your decisions. In my book *Coffee Cup Counseling* I encourage people who are in the midst of decisions involving relationships to look at the long-range consequences of their decisions. How do they affect you? If you were single and had a child, how would that decision affect your offspring? What about your family? Like it or not, your decisions do affect them. And most important of all, you must ask, "Where is God in relationship to what I am about to do?"

The greatest factor which keeps singles from establishing wholesome relationships is fear:

- fear of inadequacy
- fear of rejection
- fear of risk
- fear of sexual encounters which you are not prepared to handle
- fear of confrontation
- fear of closeness because you have been hurt
- fear of losing control
- fear of being smothered

Fear keeps you cowering in the solitary confinement of your prison of isolation. Fear has to be confronted and overcome. Instead of striving to develop relationships with everyone, be selective and focus on developing friendships with one or two individuals whom you respect. Concentrate on being the kind of person who is warm and pleasant, and from that base of comfortable friendships, you will discover that your circle of friends grows.

In the chapter which follows, I want to focus on the three major needs which confront you as a single and how those needs are met in ways which give you confidence in reaching out to people. Before we deal with that, notice the elements of a meaningful relationship, whether it is with a friend or your future mate.

1. Respect. For whatever reasons, if you lose respect for an individual, your relationship begins to rapidly disintegrate. Joan was "best friends" with Bob, the handsome guy who worked in the same department, when he took her to dinner. Then when they got back to her apartment and began watching a video, he began to caress her in ways that made her uncomfortable. "Bob, stop it. I'm not ready for this." He didn't. He ripped her blouse off, saying, "After dinner, I deserve this and I thought you wanted it, too." She didn't. She wanted him off of her and fast. When he didn't move, she began to tremble. Then, crying and yelling for help, she finally jumped to her feet, ran across the hall and beat on the door of the apartment next door. He left, and from that point on, working in the same office was unbearable.

2. *Trust.* Regardless of the level of a relationship, trust is vital. It's part of integrity which can be defined simply as "doing what you say you are going to do." A person who seldom shows up on time, doesn't call when he or she is delayed and can never be counted on to come through with the goods isn't one to develop a close relationship with. It's just that simple.

3. *Intimacy which is not to be confused with sexual contact.* My definition of intimacy is closeness, the kind of a relationship based on trust which allows you the freedom to be yourself completely without thought of rejection. My wife Darlene says (with a play on the words) it is "into-me-see." The best relationships are those which give you the freedom to completely be yourself.

As Carolyn Koons and Michael Anthony put it in *Single Adult Passages,* "What so many singles today need to realize is that intimacy can exist without sexual expression, that two people can share their thoughts and feelings without sharing their bodies. It is only when such an understanding is acknowledged that true 'intimacy'—the bonding of one soul with another—will happen freely."[10]

4. *Friendship.* "I know my boyfriend loves me," commented a young woman, adding, "but we aren't very good friends." There are times when couples have been married for many years, but for whatever reasons, they never become great friends. When someone has grown up in the kind of an environment where close relationships are

nonexistent, it is difficult for him or her to break out of the shell and reach out to anyone in genuine friendship.

5. *Emotional support.* In a quality relationship, both individuals can lean on the other for emotional support without either becoming a crutch. David and Jonathan in the Old Testament had such a relationship. When David feared for his life, Jonathan supported him, fed him privileged information and loved him as himself.

6. *Truthfulness.* "Faithful are the wounds of a friend; but the kisses of an enemy are deceitful," says Proverbs 27:6 (KJV). And what does this mean? That a friend often stabs you in the back? (Remember—with friends like that, who needs enemies?) Not so. It means that a friend values you as a person so much that he is absolutely truthful with you. The motive is love, not hostility.

7. *Reciprocal wholeness.* Good relationships are good for everyone concerned. One does not draw from the other without enriching the life of the other person so that both are better individuals than they would have been without knowing and befriending the other. It's the same balance that you see in the biblical story of David and Jonathan.

Take inventory before we go on to the next chapter. Of these five major enemies of singles, which best describes the need of your life right now (loneliness, sexual frustration, financial stability and establishing good relationships)?

On a scale of one to ten to what degree are you trusting God for His help?

Can you honestly say, "Lord, I submit my life and future to You. I'm tired of trying to sort it all out. Take my life and help me put the pieces together again"?

Am I leaning on someone presently, afraid to stand on my own?

Is fear one of the factors that keeps me from reaching out to people? If so, where does it come from and what can I do about it? Is it valid or imaginary?

Endnotes

1. Carolyn Koons and Michael Anthony, *Single Adult Passages* (Grand Rapids, MI: Baker Book House, 1991), p. 48.

2. Charles Swindoll, *Growing Strong in the Seasons of Life* (Portland, OR: Multnomah Press, 1983), as quoted in *Christianity Today*, April 1984, p. 35.

3. James L. Lynch, "Warning! Living Alone Is Dangerous to Your Health," *U.S. News and World Report*, June 30, 1980, p. 47.

4. "Loneliness termed 'worst ill,' " *The Register*, June 5, 1982, p. 14.

5. Ronald Burwell, *His*, May 1981, p. 11.

6. Ray Mossholder, *Singles Plus* (Lake Mary, FL: Creation House, 1994), p. 133.

7. Helen Roseveare, "I'm Single," *Moody Monthly*, December 1976, pp. 53-54.

8. Ibid.

9. Ronald Burwell, "The Most Important Thing in the World and Other Myths About Sex," *His*, May 1981, p. 12.

10. Koons and Anthony, p. 137.

3

What Do You Really Need?

> *"Blessed are the ears*
> *that catch the divine whisper."*
>
> —Thomas à Kempis

*A*re the needs of singles essentially the same as those of their married counterparts, or, by virtue of differences in lifestyles, buying power, relationships and friendships, do singles have unique needs?

Making the question even more personal: How would you describe the actual needs—not wants—of your life?

What do you really need to live a satisfied, complete life as a single? First, there are a lot of things which you don't need to really be content.

You don't need:

- Your own condo
- A sexy figure
- The latest fashions
- Influential friends
- Money in the bank
- A matchmaking aunt
- A cruise on the Mediterranean
- Friends who borrow money from you
- An active sex life
- A Rolex watch (even if nobody knows you bought it on a Hong Kong street)
- A convertible

But what *do* you need? When it comes to your emotional needs, I am convinced that there are three specific needs which are all interrelated in such a way that the level of your life rises or falls depending on whether one of these areas takes a hit and becomes deficient. And surprising as this may be, whether you are single or married, those needs are just the same; however (that word digs its heels into the pavement and does a 180 degree about-face), the way in which those needs are met may be much different from the way your married counterparts' needs are met.

Besides, you are not *them*. You are *you*. And this makes the whole issue intensely personal.

In the 1960s, a Catholic psychiatrist invented a new approach in dealing with the emotional needs of people. When he was in medical school, Dr. William Glasser came to the conclusion that Sigmund Freud was way off base in his approach to life and living. Glasser pioneered a new approach to psychotherapy which he called *Reality Therapy*. His book by the same title is well worth reading.

Glasser contends that when your emotional needs are met, you act in a responsible fashion. The level in your emotional tank, the thing that makes you function, is full. But when your emotional needs are not met and the level of your emotional tank drops, like a person staggering through a desert without water, you begin to do weird things which can get you into a pile of trouble. That explains very clearly why some singles find themselves in situations which wound them deeply, situations which they know are wrong, ones which seem to have no exit.

Glasser believes that every person has two basic needs:

1. To give and receive love.
2. To feel worthwhile to yourself and to others.

In simple terms, he says your two emotional needs are giving and receiving love, and self-esteem. With an overview of our spiritual natures, I'd like to add a third: a measure of security which can come only through a vertical relationship with God. That relationship serves as an anchor when the ship of your life gets pushed around in ways that threaten to beat you to death on the rocks. Let's look at these three needs from the vantage point of being single.

Need #1: To give and receive love

In the '70s Burt Bacharach and Hal David wrote a song entitled, "What the World Needs Now . . . Is Love, Sweet Love," though it was not very clear whether love involved commitment or closeness.

The late psychiatrist Karl Menninger—a man for whom I have a great deal of respect as a professional—declared, "Love is the medicine for the sickness of the world." His colleague Eric Fromm, an often-quoted psychologist, believes that loneliness and the inability to love are the underlying causes of both psychic and emotional disorders.

"There comes a time in the development of every person," says medical doctor Dr. Joshua Liebman in his book, *Peace of Mind,* "when he must love his neighbor or become a twisted, stunted personality."

"OK," you say, "We agree that love is important—not necessarily married love, or sexual love, but the kind that provides glue for relationships. But you still haven't defined what love is."

How would you define it? "Well," you say, "everybody knows what love is." Oh, yeah? When I ask an audience to define love, you should hear the "Well, love is . . . well, everybody knows what it is" kind of answers. The fact of the matter is that a lot of men think the word is spelled L-U-S-T. Defining love is like nailing jello to the wall—it isn't easily done.

In his book *Through the Looking Glass,* Lewis Carroll describes a conversation between Alice and Humpty Dumpty, who rather scornfully says, "When I use a word, it means just what I choose it to mean, neither more nor less." Alice, not content with that ambiguity, counters, "The question is whether you can make words mean different things."

Your little brother may say, "I love peanut butter sandwiches." Your dad says, "I'd love to be the CEO in our company." And you say, "I'd love to have a house of my own."

All three of you mean something different. Your brother says he loves to devour peanut butter sandwiches. You dad would like to be in control of the company. (Of course, he can do a better job running the show than the jerk who presently is there.) And you would like to own your own home.

Getting the picture? When someone declares love for you, is he or she describing a romantic emotion or a visceral response to your body? To some, love is a noun—something you give or receive. To others, it is a verb—something you do. To some love is a sacrament, holy and pure. To others, it is a lustful indulgence. It all depends on how you define the word.

In the Upper Room Jesus told the disciples that they were to love each other as He loved them (John 13:34). Pretty powerful, right? But you say, "No way. I'm not Jesus. Can't do it." For a long time I avoided the weight of those words simply because I felt that this was a benchmark, something to shoot at, but not really within my grasp to achieve.

Then I began looking at the way Jesus loved His own. There are four observations that I want to make which will help you learn to give and receive love.

Observation #1: Jesus' love was an unconditional commitment.

His love for those who walked with Him was never diminished by their personal failures or even their rejection of Him. It was never dependent upon the responses of those whom He loved. Usually people responded to the warmth of His love, but there were times when they turned and walked away from Him. Such was the young man described as the rich young ruler. A phrase recorded by Mark is powerful: "Jesus looked at him and loved him" (10:21).

Question: Have you ever loved someone, and your love was not reciprocated? You were shattered, devastated, crushed, right? What did you do? Retreat and bury the thought of love—"feelings that have died," as Paul Simon wrote?

Years ago, one of my best friends—a man that I really loved as a brother—for whatever quirky theological reasons decided that he could not be my friend (something for which he apologized twenty years later). I was disappointed and hurt. I really felt the loss. Then, the still voice of the Holy Spirit penetrated the feeling of loss, saying, "He can't stop you from loving him." Have you learned that lesson? No matter what that other person may do to you, he or she cannot stop you from the commitment to care, which is what love is about.

So much of our love is conditional—"I'll love you provided you love me back, but if you don't love me the same way I love you, it's all over. I'll take my toys and split." But Jesus' love was unconditional with no strings attached. You can and must love the same way.

Observation #2: Jesus' love was a commitment to imperfect individuals.

Take a lingering look at the idiosyncrasies and personality flaws of those who walked with Jesus. Talk about a group of socially dysfunctional individuals! Here's Peter. "Temperamental Peter," we describe him. Right—ninety percent temper, and ten percent mental. And "Doubting Thomas," a "you-gotta-show-me-if-you-want-me-to-believe" sort of guy. And then there's James and John who wanted Jesus to call down fire from heaven and wipe out those who were casting out demons in Jesus' name. Nice boys, James and John.

Consider the woman at the well of Sychar (married five times and living with a man to whom she was not married); Zaccheus—withdrawn, antisocial, probably addicted to sports; Mary and Martha, and on and on.

Everybody is imperfect. Everybody has rough spots. If you wait to love someone until he or she is perfect, forget it. It will never happen.

A single missionary by the name of Florence Alshorn went to Uganda and quickly discovered why everyone who had preceded her had eventually packed up and quit. It wasn't the cockroaches or the plague or even the headhunters who preyed in the bush. Problem #1 was the senior missionary, an extremely moody woman who wouldn't even speak to her for days at a time. Yet if Florence was to learn the language, the old girl who had single-handedly burned down villages to stop the plague was the one who had to be her teacher.

Florence almost quit.

She had every right to pack up and head home.

But she didn't.

She read First Corinthians 13 every day and prayed for the senior missionary.

You are expecting me to tell you that prayer changed the cantankerous old gal, right? I don't know for sure. But I do know that prayer changed Florence and the way she looked at her senior teacher. In her diary she wrote these touching and relevant words: "To love an individual means to accept him as he is. If you wait to love him till he has gotten rid of his faults, you are loving an idea. Love him as he is with the painful expectancy that he can be different. Only then are we loving with the love of Christ."[1]

Powerful! Do you have anybody in your world who qualifies as an "irregular person," a kind of strange eccentric, someone who is not very lovable? Take the Alshorn challenge. Read First Corinthians 13 every day and pray for that person. Do it for thirty days and see what happens.

Observation #3: Jesus' love met the needs of those who were objects of His love.

Question: How did Jesus love the Church?

Answer: He did for her what she could never do for herself. He died for her.

Lesson: Real love always puts the needs of the other above your own needs.

"If you really love me, prove it by having sex with me."

"If you really loved me, you wouldn't ask because sex without the commitment of marriage can't meet my needs or yours either."

Observation #4: Jesus' love demanded personal sacrifice.

There is a price tag attached to real love, and

that's what often makes us uncomfortable. When we look at Jesus' love, the specter of a cross looms on the horizon of our thinking. We want to receive love, not sustain pain or sacrifice in giving love to others.

Mother Teresa put it so succinctly when she said, "There can be no true love without hurt." We live in an imperfect, broken world, and to withdraw when you have sustained the pain of rejection only compounds your loneliness and depreciates your value as a person. Don't do it.

What is love? Take those four observations and put them together and you have a working definition of love: "An unconditional commitment to an imperfect person to meet the needs of that one in such a way that demands personal sacrifice."

Can you love like that? Yes, it is possible.

Something else that needs to be said: There is a great deal of difference between loving and being in love. Love is a decision, a commitment to care, and you can make that decision regardless of the temperature of your heart. Being in love with someone is great, but loving transcends the emotions and juices that attract us to each other sexually.

How do we learn to love, especially when our attempts have failed so miserably?

Your need to give and receive love was put there by God Himself, and it was also He who made provision for that need to be met—at least potentially. But our capacity to love has been lessened by quick fixes and fractured, broken relationships. Pulling back, we stifle the flow of God's love through us to those about us. The Bible makes it clear that God is the source of all love (1 John 4:8), and that His love flows through our lives as the result of the indwelling Holy Spirit (Romans 8:5).

If the level on your love tank has dropped—possibly even gone almost flat—pray something like this: "Lord Jesus, I've been so hurt that I've pulled in the bridge, but I want You to touch my life with Your love. Make it so definite that I can reach out and love others beginning today." You'll be amazed at what happens. It's the only solution to a tough issue.

Need #2: *To feel worthwhile to yourself and to others*

One of the saddest letters that has come to me in the more than three decades of broadcasting was one written by a single woman in her sixties who had suffered all her life from low self-esteem. Here's her story.

When she was born, her mother either could not raise her or chose not to. At birth the little infant was placed in an orphanage. As she grew into childhood, she became painfully aware that she was different. Periodically prospective parents would come to view the children. The attendants would dress them in their best clothes, line them up (about like you would if you were showing your dog in an animal show) and then the adopting parents would pick a child. Repeatedly, the little girl was left behind.

As she was growing up, the message she got was: "You have to be a good girl if you ever expect to be adopted." Finally, at age twelve, it happened. At last, she had her own mother and father, but even then she seemed to feel that acceptance with her new family was based on how good she was. That persistent, nagging feeling was there, "You can never be good enough."

As a teenager, she went to church and heard the gospel. At the invitation, she responded and came forward to accept the Lord as her personal Savior. That night she went home and prayed that God would let her die! *Just a minute,* you may be thinking, *wasn't she happy to know that she was God's child?* Not so, in this case. She felt that she could never be good enough for God to love her so her only alternative was to pray that she would die and go straight to heaven while her record was clear.

Then in her letter to me she asked if God performs plastic surgery of the heart to take away the scars of childhood.

Question: How good must you be for God to love you?

The fact is that your goodness or even your badness has nothing to do with the answer. In Paul's letter to the Ephesians, he made it very clear that our acceptance before God is not a matter of our goodness—what we do, or don't do—but is based on what Jesus Christ did.

How is this important when it comes to a sense of personal fulfillment in life? Very important. An understanding of who you are directly relates to how you feel about yourself and other people.

Joann was an attractive young woman who worked at Clark Air Force Base in the Philippines. Her father was an American serviceman, her mother a Filipina living in nearby Angeles City. When her mother became pregnant with her, neither the father or mother wanted the child. The man who impregnated her mother eventually was shipped out, but not before he made an indelible impression on the little girl who vividly remembers his telling her, "You are no good! You've got bad blood in you!" I spent weeks working with this young woman who had a nice personality and was a capable secretary but kept prospective suitors at arm's length because she didn't think she was good enough for them.

How impressionable is a young child? Very. Growing up, children don't understand how important they are in the sight of God. They only know that they are not as bright as their brother or sister or the neighbor's child. They quickly become victims of the sarcastic comments of other children.

"Fatty fatty two-by-four, can't get through the kitchen door." "Sticks and stones may break my bones," we hurl back, "but words can never hurt me." Lie! They go to the very core of our being. When we grow up without being loved—even if it is by one person who makes a difference in our life—we struggle with self-image, usually feeling that we are inferior to everybody else. That person who makes a difference should be a parent, but can be anyone: an aunt or uncle, a teacher, a friend, a pastor.

Actor Marlon Brando, known for his tough and violent roles, says that as a boy growing up he rarely received a word of praise from his alcoholic mother. In his autobiography, however, Brando says that there was one person in his life who made a difference: a shop teacher. The two years that Brando spent in Lathrop Intermediate School in Santa Ana, California helped him to think differently about himself. There the youthful Brando met Burton Rowley, now deceased; but more than that, Rowley made Brando feel important. He helped him believe in himself, and made him think he could do something with his life that counted. Writes Brando, "His words of encouragement affect me to this day."

I couldn't help thinking of how our comments influence the lives of people as I recently played golf with a friend. I spend far more time working than playing golf—my game isn't exactly marvelous. On that particular day, a drive got away from me and my ball headed for a condominium near the fairway. Following a rather loud crash which I first thought meant my ball had gone through a glass window, a man came running out of the door waving a towel, yelling as loudly as he could.

I told my golfing companion, "I bet I broke his window. Let's go see."

When we got there, I inquired as to the damage.

"No," said the annoyed resident, "you didn't hit my window. Your ball hit my roof."

"Any damage?" I asked.

"No," he said, but then he quickly added, "You know something? You're a terrible golfer!" That insight really made my day. I knew my game was not very good. But playing as seldom as I do, I have to settle for bogey golf or worse. I smiled at that insight—"You're a terrible golfer." I wondered if that man had that attitude with his family and children.

Louis Zamperini believes that a single individual can make a difference in the life of a troubled teenager. You see, he's been there. He learned to run the practical way—fleeing from the Torrance, California police where he grew up. Zamperini went on to earn a gold medal in the Olympics as a runner. In World War II, he was shot down and spent fifty-two days on a life raft in the Pacific. Finally rescued by the Japanese, he was put in a prisoner of war camp. When they learned he was a former medalist in the Olympics, he was forced to run against the finest Japanese athletes in a display of mockery.

After the war Zamperini began working with juveniles—tough street kids. He believed that every kid not only needs someone to believe in him or her, but that every kid is going to get thrills one way or another—legitimately or the wrong way, as he himself had done. Taking youths to the mountains, he began to teach them climbing skills. Zamperini discovered that a street tough kid became a whimpering pup when it came time to rappel down the face of a cliff. Zamperini would tell them, "Look, you can do this. I know you can, and if you don't do it, I'm gonna throw you over." They learned!

Can one person make much of a difference? Dr. William Glasser writes,

> We must be involved with other people, one at the very minimum, but hopefully more than one. At all times in our lives, we must have at least one person who cares for us and whom we care for ourselves. If we do not have this person, we will not be able to fulfill our basic needs. . . . One characteristic is essential in the other person: he must be in touch with reality himself and able to fulfill his own needs within the world.[2]

Glasser also did extensive work with juveniles and discovered that at the root of many troubled lives was the fact nobody was there who really made a person believe, "You can do it; I've got faith in you!" Today vast numbers of juveniles have found their identity in gangs when they didn't find it at home.

For you who struggle with this issue, I have several comments:

It's OK to believe in yourself.

When you come to understand that you are a

unique individual created in the image of God, you free yourself of two hang-ups that haunt people who do not understand their importance in the sight of God: feelings of inferiority and attitudes of superiority, both of which you compensate for by thinking you are inadequate. In recent days a lot has been written from a Christian perspective that denigrates an understanding of your uniqueness. Saying that to believe in yourself is pride or ego, authors have charged that we must consider ourselves to be nothing.

Yet simple logic would tell you that if you take an ordinary clay vase which is worth practically nothing and place diamonds and emeralds in that vase, the net worth has just skyrocketed. The Bible says simply that when you became a believer, Jesus Christ came to indwell your life. "But we have this treasure in jars of clay," writes Paul, "to show that this all-surpassing power is from God and not from us" (2 Corinthians 4:7).

At the same time, remember that Jesus talked about loving our neighbor as ourselves without even suggesting that to recognize your value and worth in the sight of God is wrong.

Who said you are inferior? God doesn't. He considers you to be an individual with unique gifts and talents. Eleanor Roosevelt, a woman who had more than a few personal struggles in her own life, including the realization that the affection of her husband was shared with another woman, said that no one can make you feel inferior unless you let it happen. She's right.

Understand that singleness is not defectiveness.

"My daughter is almost thirty. Would you talk with her to see what's the matter with her that she hasn't found the right young man?"

Believe it or not, parents still make those kind of requests. Generally when that happens, I discover the young woman is a college graduate, holding down a good job and is far superior to the suitors who have bored her with their clumsy efforts to court her. To pressure her into marriage would not only be demeaning but a real injustice to her.

Will we ever learn that singleness is not defectiveness? In their book *Single Person's Identity,* John Fischer and Lia Fuller O'Neill describe the dilemma of many singles:

> The suggestion creeps into the back of my mind that I'm incomplete. I'm in a holding pattern. I'm flying around trying to find the airport so that I can get my feet on the ground and start living. This type of thinking keeps me from living *now*, to be what God has called me to be. It can be very subtle. It comes up in the way I keep my room. I keep thinking . . . "when" . . . "when" I have my own place . . . or "when" I have someone with me, *then* I'll do this or that.[3]

Society contributes to this defectiveness syndrome by the emphasis on couples. Some of it, I suppose, is to be expected. The family is the basis of our social structure, and parents as a twosome find it very convenient to invite other couples for dinner, parties and activities. But are not singles also part of the family? Are they to be excluded as an appendage, a fifth wheel, an oddity? Not on your life. You may live in a couples' world, but you don't have to let this kind of defective thinking influence you. An individual who is married is not more complete than one who is single. Marriage does not make a female a "real woman" nor does having sexual intercourse with someone make a "real man" out of a male. Wholeness is the result of understanding how you feel about yourself, knowing that you are complete or incomplete only in relationship to your thinking, not your marital status.

Realize that worth is not devalued by your need.

Are there individuals who "need" to get married? Of course! Only someone with one oar out of the water would deny that. For that reason Paul told the Corinthians to marry. The single life is not for everyone, just as marriage is not for everyone. But if you are one of those individuals who needs a mate and you are waiting on God's timing, understand that your worth as a person is not depreciated or lessened by your need.

Yet when you have a need and that need is not met, you may—even without realizing what you are doing—establish a relationship which you think will meet that need. It doesn't. You only end up with frustration.

Teresa was like that. Growing up in a home without a father and living with a mother who was gone much of the time, Teresa, seventeen, liked the attention of Mark, a young man, age twenty-six, who worked in the same plant. When Mark began to walk her home in the evenings, something began to happen inside. She felt a warmth and experienced an intimate feeling which was new and exciting. It was not sexual, as she described it. "Mark made me feel important," she explained, adding, "something which nobody ever did before."

When their relationship began to intensify, he wanted more physical contact than walking hand in hand together. She didn't. But neither did she want to lose his attention, and though she knew what she was doing violated her sense of right and wrong, she did it anyway justifying that "he loves me." Now she tells me that she is having his baby, and though they hope to marry sometime, "he loves me too much to marry me now." Figure that one out!

For some girls, having a baby gives them a temporary sense of worth. "Look, isn't she beautiful? That's *my* baby!" And in the mind of the girl who had never completed high school but had become a mother at eighteen, giving birth to an infant was the first accomplishment she had ever made. This leads us to one more observation.

Don't confuse the desire for a warm, loving relationship with sexuality.

"The choice of single people to sleep with dates," says Stephanie Brandon, "has much less to do with lust than it does with the simple human need of being touched."

As I am writing this section, my wife of thirty-five years and I are separated—at least, temporarily. She'll be home in a couple of weeks. Right now she is helping our daughter who just presented us with our fourth grandchild. But what I miss the most is the companionship, the soft touch of her hand, the knowledge that she is there, that I can say anything I want and know that she will love and accept me. That, of course, is the heart of a relationship. Question: Must you be married to have that kind of a relationship?

Before you decide, let me tell you about an experience that Elisabeth Elliot had when she was visiting Dohnavur Fellowship in South India. While she was there doing research for her book on Amy Carmichael, she met a remarkable woman who was working with the mentally incompetent. The staff member herself was greatly handicapped by the loss of one eye. "I have no professional training," she explained. "The Holy Spirit gives me new wisdom each day to deal with them. Some are like wild animals, but the Lord Himself is my helper. I can't see on one side, but even in my weakness He has helped me."

When Elisabeth Elliot inquired as to how she had

become involved in such a work, Pungaja explained that one day, tremendously burdened by life, she went to Amy Carmichael, who was affectionately known as "Amma" by nationals of India. "When she hugged me," she said, "all my burdens went away!" The Indian men and women who followed in her footsteps, serving others, have been a powerful witness to the life of Amy Carmichael. "When she hugged me, all my burdens went away!"

Is it any wonder that the suffering and neglected of our world will line up for this kind of love? Have you ever considered what kind of difference a touch of your love could make in someone's life? People are all around you waiting for that kind of a loving relationship. Try calling your local hospital to volunteer in the nursery. Visit a retirement community and ask the social director for the names of people there with no relatives and then drop by for a visit. Or take a look at your contemporaries to see who needs love.

It just takes one person who believes in you to make a difference!

In recent years, medical science has discovered that there is healing in the power of a touch. Karl Menninger, the renowned psychiatrist quoted earlier, has demonstrated that mentally retarded individuals respond far more when there is some physical contact between them and their therapists. An article published in a medical journal pointed out that patients with heart attacks stabilize far more quickly when someone who loves them is present to hold their hand. It has also been demonstrated that cerebral palsy victims move more normally after receiving sensory stimulation.

People respond to the loving touch. A family counselor says that most unwanted teenage pregnancies could be prevented if a father only hugged his teenage daughter every day. "Three hugs a day" is the prescription for good mental health.

A phone company encouraged subscribers to use their long distance service by advertising, "Reach out and touch someone." That's applied Christianity. Yes, in love, reach out and touch someone today.

Need #3: To have security that comes through a relationship with God

"I have been a Christian for more than four years and knowing Jesus has allowed me to not only accept but enjoy my singleness."—Bill

Long ago Augustine—a man who lived a rather loose life as a single—eventually became an apologist for the faith and one of the church fathers. He wrote, "Thou hast made us for thyself, O God, and our heart is restless until it finds its rest in thee." Have you ever asked yourself why men and women have a wedding ceremony when they come together in marriage? Why not just live together as a lot of people do?

Marriage involves far more than just sex. Animals court, then copulate and bear offspring, but you were made in the image of God and endowed with a soul. Among the reasons why couples commit themselves to each other in marriage is the recognition of our spiritual natures.

When you really commit yourself to the Lord and establish the kind of a relationship with Him whereby you take seriously what He says in His Word and strive to live for Him, there comes a strength in your life which is like a gyroscope that holds you steady in the storm.

Within your heart is an emptiness, a space which only the Creator can really inhabit. What I am describing is not a "head knowledge" but a "heart relationship." We live in an imperfect, broken world and, at times, you will feel the brunt of all that imperfection. You will be misunderstood; you will be jilted by someone you considered to be your "best friend"; you will have disappointments which you feel you don't deserve.

Understanding that you are still God's child and you have a connection with the Father gives you One to whom you can pour out your heart, One to whom you can turn in times of loneliness and difficulty.

One of the reasons that I so love the Psalms is that I see in them the whole gamut of human emotions—love, disappointment, hate, rejection, fear, hope and a great deal more in a vast panorama of feelings. Consistent throughout this compilation of songs is the theme that God is a Refuge to whom we can run, a Shelter in the storm, a Friend who understands when all others fail us.

The night after we brought our firstborn home

from the hospital was an evening I shall never forget. My wife Darlene almost died in childbirth, and after a hospital stay of about a week, she was still confined to her bed. About 2 a.m. Bonnie, whose life was also threatened, began to cry. And the longer she cried, the more desperate both of us became. Two hours later I called the hospital. I explained the desperation of the situation and asked if I could go back to the hospital and get the bottle of formula that we had inadvertently forgotten.

"No, I'm sorry there is nothing we can do. Call your doctor at 8 o'clock in the morning."

I thought, *I doubt that this baby will live until 8 o'clock in the morning, and I* know *that I won't!*

I was on my own. I took that little bundle in my arms and walked the floor, and that night I learned my first lesson of parenting. I discovered that when I wrapped the blanket rather tightly around her and held her snugly in my arms, she began to settle down and was secure.

Often I see the same insecurity in those who are a long way from the Father. Take Peter, for example, as a case study in security. The farther Peter was from Jesus, the more insecure he was. Inversely, the closer He was to the Lord, the more secure he was. In your mind's eye, visualize Peter as he was in the courtyard of the house of Caiaphas after Jesus was taken in Gethsemane. He wanted to be where Jesus was in spite of the physical danger which resulted from the association.

One of the disturbing marks of life today is the

vast number of people—both singles and marrieds—who confess to faith in Jesus Christ, yet
when it comes to their morals and business eth-
ics, there is practically no difference between the
believer who goes to church with regularity and
the nonbeliever who is indifferent to spiritual
matters. Research indicates that there is almost
as much sexual expression among singles who
consider themselves to be Christians as among
non-Christians. Couples tell me, "We're living
together," and then as we talk and I inquire
about a relationship with Jesus Christ, they candidly say, "Oh, yes. We're Christians."

When the disciples were having a problem with
the issue of consistency, Jesus challenged, "Why
do you call me, 'Lord, Lord,' and do not do what I
say?" (Luke 6:46). For centuries sexual intercourse apart from marriage has been considered to
be sin, not simply having sex with the same person in a "loving relationship."

When the woman confronted Jesus at the well
of Sychar (John 4), He told her that she had had
four husbands, and the one she was living with
was not her husband. He didn't consider the "de
facto" relationship to be the equivalent of marriage. In Revelation 21:8, John mentions "sexually
immoral" along with a pretty despicable catalog of
vices as those who will have their place "in the
fiery lake of burning sulfur." Not too pleasant a
thought.

Sure, God forgives sin. That isn't the issue. The
point I am making is that you need a live, mean-

ingful relationship with God, the kind that comes as you strive to do God's will. I'm not talking about perfection; I'm talking about commitment, forsaking the kind of a lifestyle which may be in vogue but is not in keeping with our Father's will. And with that comes a vibrant faith which gives you a psychological and spiritual anchor that makes a difference in your life.

Can These Needs Be Met As a Single?

Do you remember the words of Paul which we talked about in chapter 2?

> I know what it is to be in need, and I know what it is to have plenty. I have learned the secret of being content in any and every situation, whether well fed or hungry, whether living in plenty or in want. I can do everything through him who gives me strength. (Philippians 4:12-13)

God would have had a cruel sense of humor, as some suggest, to create us in such a way that our sexual desires leave us totally frustrated unless He had given us a means of coping with temptation, of dealing with our emotional needs, of finding fulfillment, whether it is by bringing someone into our lives who is a companion and friend or a mate who meets those needs. For that, we must trust Him.

Endnotes

1. J.H. Oldham, *Florence Alshorn*, pp. 22-29, as quoted by Vernon Grounds in "The Love Which Enables and Transforms." Monograph distributed for class notes, Denver Seminary, January 1963.

2. William Glasser, *Reality Therapy* (New York: Harper & Row, 1965), p. 7.

3. John Fischer and Lia Fuller O'Neill, *Single Person's Identity* (Palo Alto, CA: Discover Publishing, 1973), pp. 1-2.

4

The Power of Positive Decisions

"An obstacle is like the hurdle
in a steeplechase—ride up to it . . .
throw your heart over it . . .
and the horse will go along, too."

—Unknown

*A*n acquaintance of mine was the first officer on a PT boat in World War II. When the vessel took a hit from enemy gunfire and began to sink, the radio operator immediately sent out an SOS: "We are sinking. Request immediate help!"

The nearest ship was also engaged in battle and sent back the reply, "Unable to assist at the present time."

A second message was sent, "We are sinking; must have immediate help!"

Back came a negative reply: "Unable to assist. Do the best you can!"

The men aboard frantically bailed water and plugged holes. In a few minutes the first officer ordered the following message sent: "We have decided not to sink!"

There is something about that spirit that appeals to me in a day when I see so much negative thinking.

- "I'm mad at God. He didn't send me a husband."
- "I don't know what to do. Every girl I date thinks that I want to get married."

To marry or not to marry may not be a choice. Some desperately would like to marry, but no one takes that person seriously. However, the attitude with which you respond is a choice, a decision which you make. Some singles have an amazing amount of negative feelings toward the Lord because He has not sent the right person into their lives. They are angry with God.

What does God really owe you? Does He owe you a husband who makes a good income, drives a nice car, has a wonderful personality and is well liked by associates? Does He owe you a beautiful girl who has a nice personality, a figure to match, a love for children and beautiful eyes? Strange, isn't it, that we lead ourselves to conclude God has failed if our dreams and hopes don't materialize exactly as we had thought they would? "I asked God for a husband," said one young woman, "and He sent me an electric blanket."

Sometimes God loves you so much that He spares you from yourself. Twenty years from now you may go to your high school class reunion and talk with the girl who could once make you dizzy with only a glance, and you may say, "God, thank You for loving me so much that she ignored me." Waiting for God's timing is one of the most difficult tasks that you will ever face in life. Most of our mistakes in life are the result of getting ahead of God.

Timing is everything!

Meanwhile, God's sustaining help (the Bible calls it grace) is there to help you. How you respond to circumstances is your decision.

You can determine that this week you will limit your time for feeling sorry for yourself to:

- thirty seconds
- thirty minutes
- thirty hours

Then you decide to get on with your life. Every single is confronted with five choices which result in five major decisions that have everything to do with peace of mind or constant unrest and frustration.

Choice #1: Bitterness or release

Businessman and entrepreneur Ted Turner says he is looking forward to going to hell "because," he says, "that's where I belong."[1] His remarks, made at a Baptist church luncheon, made hair curl on little ladies who hadn't heard such spicy comments for a long while. And what caused Turner to become bitter toward God?

His world started collapsing when his sister died.

His parents' marriage failed.

Finally his dad committed suicide.

And then Turner cried out, "Why did You allow this to happen to me, God?" In anger, bitterness and pain, he turned his back on God.

When you are confronted with the pain of disappointment—your boyfriend ends up marrying your best friend, your girlfriend says, "No way, José!" or your dog dies—one of two things will happen. The disappointment will drive you to the Lord where you cry out for help, or else you will become bitter. And bitterness will begin to kill you.

The real issue is simple: Is God responsible for all your disappointments in life? Can we hold Him accountable for the storms which drive your ship onto the rocks or blame Him for the failure of the doctor to diagnose properly your mother's illness? Shall we charge Him with neglect when your fiancé is killed in an accident because an automobile mechanic failed to connect the drive-shaft properly?

God ends up being a whipping boy charged with the responsibility for all our failures and disappointments. Think for a moment what would happen if God spared His children from all disappointment so that only those who do not know Him suffer the pain and sorrow that disappointment brings. Millions would "convert" to avoid the difficulty. If God spared His children from difficulty, loving Him as a conscious choice would be less meaningful because we could never be sure of our motive.

The verb "choose" appears about fifty-nine times in the Bible (depending on the translation you consult). A study of those references suprisingly reveals that in most cases the writers record what God chose to do. Yet a significant number of these references refer to choices which people made. For example, Moses led the children of Israel to the edge of the Promised Land and gave them this charge:

> This day I call heaven and earth as witnesses against you that I have set before

> you life and death, blessings and curses.
> Now choose life, so that you and your
> children may live and that you may love
> the LORD your God, listen to his voice,
> and hold fast to him. . . . (Deuteronomy
> 30:19-20)

Your response to what you do not like or understand is a choice: bitterness or blessing. Joshua, Moses' successor, made a decision, saying, ". . . As for me and my household, we will serve the LORD" (Joshua 24:15).

In the words of people like Ted Turner, who choose to blame God for disappointments in life, I detect a sad note of remorse, like the lament of a little child who when disciplined by his mother responds, "I hate you!" without understanding the meaning of that phrase. More honestly Turner should say, "I don't like what happened; I can't understand it. I'm angry about the whole matter." But his hostility should be directed at the loss, not at God.

God understands that kind of pain. When confronted with bitter disappointments, David cried out, "Why are you downcast, O my soul? Why so disturbed within me? Put your hope in God, for I will yet praise him, my Savior and my God" (Psalm 42:11).

A certain young woman, bitten by a dog suspected of having rabies, was immediately rushed to a hospital where she was treated and left in an adjacent room until it could be determined whether or not the dog had the disease. As you probably know, treatment for rabies is painful and expensive. If it can be determined that an animal is not infected, the victim is spared a great deal of discomfort and anxiety. An intern on duty explained the seriousness of the situation to the woman and then was called to other duties.

Passing by the room a short while later, the young doctor noticed that the woman would stare in space and mutter to herself, visibly shaken by the trauma of what had happened. He also noticed that the woman was writing something. He thought she was possibly writing her will or funeral instructions. *This has really gotten to her,* he thought. So certain was he that she was taking it much too seriously that he went in to comfort her.

"Are you writing your will?" asked the young doctor.

"Oh, no!" she replied.

"Funeral instructions?"

Again she shook her head. Then she explained: "Just in case I do have rabies, I'm making a list of the men I want to bite before I die."

We smile at the thought of such a thing taking place, but daily people poison their systems with hatred and revenge. I'm thinking of a letter from a woman who was bitter about the loss of the one she loved to another woman. She closed by saying, "I now have nothing to live for but revenge."

"The sweet taste of revenge," some call it, but in reality, there is nothing sweet about the bitterness of revenge. I have known people who lived for years with the burden of hatred, waiting their time to take revenge on an enemy. Surprisingly, Christians are not immune from the desire to take revenge on their enemies, either.

To harbor bitterness and hatred toward an individual who has wronged you is only natural; to forgive is supernatural. Twice in the New Testament God emphasizes forgiveness, "Vengeance is mine; I will repay, saith the Lord" (Romans 12:19, KJV). When He was crucified, instead of taking vengeance upon His enemies, Christ cried out, "Father, forgive them; for they know not what they do" (Luke 23:34, KJV).

If ever a man had the right to seek vengeance, it would have been Joseph, whose brothers sold him into slavery because they were jealous of the love his father had for him. But instead of awaiting his time for vengeance, he blessed his brothers who came seeking his help. You can read about it in Genesis chapters 37-50 in the Old Testament. Joseph explained why he refused the path of vengeance: "And as for you, you meant evil against me, but God meant it for good" (50:20, NASB). In other words, "You meant it for evil, to hurt me, but God used it for good to save many lives."

What's wrong with vengeance? First, God says because of your own failures and frailties, you have no right to vengeance. He'll settle the score without your help. Second, unforgiveness stunts your growth spiritually. Third, hatred and bitterness are poisons that physically hurt you. When you become filled with bitterness, you are the real loser.

How do you deal with bitterness when it has loomed larger than life? Just forget it? It doesn't work that way. There is, however, a way—the power of your decision to release that bitterness and give it to the Lord. You can come and say, "Father God, I know my bitterness is wrong. It's killing me. I can't sleep. I am filled with anger and hatred. I give this to You. Please take it and let Your love fill my heart. I release it right now."

In Second Corinthians Paul talks about bringing every thought into captivity to the obedience of Jesus Christ (see 2 Corinthians 10:5). You can do that. Does it work? Yes!

Before we go on to the next section, I want to relate a true story about a single friend I have, a man that I have grown to love and respect. To protect him, as well as those who are involved, I have changed his name, but the facts are painfully accurate in every detail.

During World War II, William was a little boy, barely old enough to remember when the Japanese came and seized his father, sending him to prison and accusing his mother of being a spy. Far from being a spy, his mother had come to China as a missionary, had married a Chinese businessman and had remained in China to be near her husband and family when the communist forces of Mao Tse-tung overthrew the government.

Because of their Christian faith, the mother, along with her children, were placed under house arrest and for many years were virtual prisoners with meager rations year after year, barely above starvation subsistence.

"If it's the last thing I do," vowed William, "I will seek out the Japanese who imprisoned my father and get my revenge." Then as William grew older he came to realize that revenge is not really in keeping with the teaching of Christ. He finally gave up the idea of taking a life, but the bitterness was still there. He knew the name of the man who had sent his father to prison and the city in Japan where he lived. "The least I can do," he reasoned, "is to go to his place of employment and expose his war crimes and embarrass him, paying him back for the suffering and humiliation he caused my family."

William's long awaited payday finally came. Immediately prior to Teng Hsiao-p'ing's trip to the United States, a number of Chinese were allowed to leave the mainland as a good-will gesture. William was one of them. He first went to Japan where he determined to find the man who had caused his family to suffer.

According to his plan, Tokyo was his first stop. He was met at the airport and taken to the home of a friend, and during the next few days, William picked up a book that changed his rendezvous with revenge. It had been written by a Dutch woman he had never heard of, a woman whose name was Corrie ten Boom. What he read touched his heart. In her book Corrie told of her experience of being taken from her home and put in a concentration camp at Ravensbruck. She related how God had eventually delivered her and then she had returned to Germany with the message that forgiveness is the only answer to bitterness and revenge.

Corrie told how after speaking to a group, she had been confronted by one of the SS guards from the very prison where she had faced death hour by hour. The guard thrust forth his hand, saying he too had become a believer and that God had forgiven him. "Forgive me, fraulein," said the guard with his hand outstretched.

As Corrie wrote how God in that instance touched her heart and made her realize that she too must forgive, God began speaking to William's heart. God began to reprove him for the attitude which he knew was wrong, and the bitterness and hatred began to subside. The mission of revenge was forsaken.

One closing thought. Bitterness may not send you across oceans or continents, but it can surely send you into a tailspin when it comes to your own spiritual life. Just as God met Corrie ten Boom and the friend I described today, He can meet you. Bitterness will kill you. "Father," said Jesus, "forgive them." And so must you.

Choice #2: Sexual purity or "I'll take my chances!"

In the film version of Tom Clancey's novel *Clear and Present Danger,* there is a scene where the hero, Jack Ryan, takes a strong stand against the politics of expediency. Confronted with an angry antagonist, Ryan holds out for what he believes is moral and right. But the antagonist, Ritter, counters, "Jack, you're a boy scout!" Ryan turns and walks away as Ritter hurls the angry words, "Gray! The world is gray, Jack!"

Is he right? Has the world become gray with the lines of demarcation wiped out between black and white, right and wrong, moral and immoral? Are we the final arbiters of all of this, or is there still a moral right and wrong, dictated long ago by the God of heaven who sent His Son to show us the way through the moral jungle which confronts us today?

Shortly before his death, historian Arnold Toynbee said that those of us who are going to be knocking on the door of the twenty-first century are unique to all mankind. He said, "We are the first generation of man to try to build a society without a moral reference point."

Scary, isn't it?

One of the spin-offs of the complexity of life today is the fact that decisions are thrust upon you which you did not ask for and would prefer not to make, but by virtue of the moral climate in which you live, you have to decide—one way or the other.

Your choices are often made on the basis of your desires, and your desires are a reflection of what you really are. It is in this world of sometimes difficult choices that you find yourself as a believer often groping for the right way but seldom considering that God may have a will for you which runs contrary to your biological instincts as well as the social pressure of your peers.

Craig Ellison wrote in the *Alliance Witness* (now *Alliance Life*), "All too many of us who call ourselves God's people live like functional atheists. We make many of our choices without even considering what God's view is. We become conformed to our culture, rather than being transformers of it."

Scores of people—possibly you, too—are simply not aware of what God's direction is when it comes to making decisions. Seldom would they put themselves in direct opposition to His will. They just don't know (and sometimes would prefer not to know). If there is one thing that the Bible makes clear, it is that God wills your sexual purity. Here's how Paul put it: "For God wants you to be holy and pure, and to keep clear of all sexual sin" (1 Thessalonians 4:3, TLB).

I have lived through the sexual revolution of the '60s when society said, "As long as you both agree, go ahead and do it; it's your own business." Sexual mores changed. Then came the '70s and the '80s when people began to realize that sex—especially for women—is not simply a matter of a physical relationship. It involves the totality of your being—your emotions, your outlook on life, your memories, your very soul.

Gradually people began to realize that something vital was missing in relationships—the element of commitment. As Rick Steadman put it, "The sexual revolution promised happiness, freedom, and intimacy, but the real result was the gradual cheapening of a sense of personal value and a sense of sexual value among single adults— and even among married adults who were sexually permissive before marriage."[2]

Recently I read everything I could find in print on singles, and the vast majority of secular publications assume (contrary to reality) that all singles are either sexually active or looking for a sexual partner. Some, however, more realistically understand that the sexual revolution has backfired. Rather than a fear of an unwanted pregnancy or of contracting AIDS, the reason behind the abstinence of these singles is the realization that casual sexual relations cannot meet their deep emotional needs. The greatest losers are women, because unlike their male partners, their sexual satisfaction includes their whole outlook on life, not simply a physical orgasm.

Others such as Carolyn See in *Cosmopolitan* magazine are asking the hard questions. In an article entitled, "The New Chastity," she says, "Sex is supposed to be fun, freeing . . . yet too many partners can sometimes make you feel disconsolate, unsatisfied. Why are so many young women suddenly swearing off the world of 'junk food' sex?" She then answers her own question:

> Yet, however difficult the choice, after close to two decades of sexual permissiveness (what a tiresome phrase; one gets "permission" to go to the cloak-

room in grade school, not to go to bed with darling men!), more and more young woman are opting for the new chastity. . . . "What's all this stuff about the new chastity?" asks a beautiful showgirl who was once married to a famous tap dancer. I'm still working on the old kind! Save yourself for a man you love or at least one who makes your heart flutter. Otherwise it's meat love, under brand X catsup."[3]

The great experiment hasn't worked.

The things men and women most want out of male-female relationships are very different. What women want is intimacy; what men want is good sex. When both are willing to trade some for the other (that is, men are willing to allow a certain amount of vulnerability provided they get better sex for it, and women are willing to give sex in the hopes of intimacy), neither can find real satisfaction apart from the commitment of marriage.

Why hasn't the great experiment in casual sex worked? Mary Ann Mayo in her book *A Christian Guide to Sexual Counseling* contends that singles confuse sex with intimacy. "Scarcely does the person seeking intimacy through sex relate their [sic] emptiness, complications and health problems back to their source: sex with no commitment."[4] Sexual relations without commitment is like candy which tastes good but isn't good for you. Your needs can't be met.

Sex therapist Shirley Zussman says that her patients complain about the emptiness of sex without commitment. "Being part of a meat market is appalling in terms of self-esteem," she says. "Fears, of both loneliness and intimacy, are a backlash against the 'cool sex' promoted during the sexual revolution."[5]

In an article focusing on the dangers of casual sex, *U.S. News and World Report* quotes a young woman, age thirty, who is an advertising executive. She reflects the concern of her gender when she says,

> Sometimes, right before I ask a guy up to my apartment for a drink, I look at him and ask myself, "Is this guy worth two weeks on penicillin?" Most of the time, I have to say no. That's why I'm looking for a guy to settle down with, to finally make that kind of question moot.[6]

Psychiatrist Henry Abraham agrees. He says, "We are now seeking a balance. We realize that revolving-door sex is not the answer to true love and commitment. . . . After all, a roll in the hay does not a sexual relationship make."[7]

In the '80s masses of young singles found someone "to settle down with," but lacking the commitment of marriage, they didn't stay settled for long. Of every 100 couples who live together without the blessing of marriage, 60 of the 100 will break up before they marry. Of the 40 remaining who eventually do get to the altar, only 18 will establish lasting relationships—a significant fewer number than the norm.

How important is the element of commitment in a relationship? It is the glue that makes relationships work over a long period of time. But there can be no real discussion of commitment without commitment to marry, to go public. Otherwise, what is the duration of commitment?

- As long as you pay your half of the rent and the food?
- As long as we both shall agree?
- As long as I can't find anyone more beautiful than you?
- As long as you keep on supporting me?
- Or what?

Without the commitment of marriage, two people are never completely relaxed. They never fully let down their guard. Both are playing games, which is why sexual adjustment after marriage is much greater for those who have lived together previously. Why? Before marriage she thinks: "If I don't give him what he wants, he's liable to leave me, and I can't stand the rejection and pain of his walking out on me."

He thinks: "I had better put on my best behavior or else she may close the door to what I want." Then they marry. The charades are off. That which previously was "forbidden fruit" becomes legitimate and loses its thrill.

In the '70s Dr. Joyce Brothers was an advocate of cautious sex. Surprising some of her colleagues, she openly touted the benefits of living together. Then she changed her mind and wisely said, in effect, "This just doesn't work!" In a 1985 article published in *New Woman* magazine, Dr. Brothers listed the following reasons that living together apart from marriage doesn't work:

- Divorce may be more likely later (an eighty percent higher chance).
- There is a lower level of satisfaction after marriage.
- Men move in primarily for sex.
- Few marriages actually result from cohabitation.
- There is a higher risk of sexual disease.
- Sexual hostility is symptomatic.
- Cohabiting women feel less secure.
- Breaking up is just as painful.[8]

When someone says to you, "Move in with me. That's the only way we will find out if we are compatible," you had better think twice. Not only do you put yourself in defiance of what God wills for your life because He knows it won't work, but you also have to realize your chances for a lasting marriage are minuscule.

"Well, you never buy a shoe without trying it on. How will we know if we are compatible?" some say. But we aren't buying shoes, remember? We're talking about relationships.

But we are just human!

That sex is explosive isn't questioned. With that thought still in your mind, picture the situation I am about to describe. A certain young man, probably in his late twenties, is employed by a wealthy man who, over a period of time, entrusts everything he owns or controls to this individual—the other employees, his equipment, even the financial control of his business. Everything is under the direction of this charming, handsome young man.

While the owner of the business is away, his wife begins to notice how good-looking and charming the young man is. She is lonely and longs for companionship. *Spending the night with him,* she begins to reason, *would certainly be better than being alone.* So she invites him to have dinner, and the invitation makes it clear that she has a good deal more in mind than dinner.

Be honest with me! If you were that young man, lonely and separated from your family and native country, how would you react? "What you would do if you could do, in the sight of God you have already done!" says the old aphorism.

The situation that I just described took place hundreds of years ago, though it could well have been re-enacted in the place where you live. You can read all about it in the Bible, chapter 39 of the book of Genesis. The young man whom I described was known as Joseph, and his temptress was the wife of Potiphar, a ruler in Egypt. The reaction of this man and how he faced sexual temptation provides insights that can help you when temptation comes knocking on your door.

The first and obvious fact that stares us in the face is that Joseph did not rationalize or justify what he undoubtedly would have found pleasure in doing. He could have said, "Nobody will ever know what I am doing. Morality is a very private matter."

A second observation from Joseph's experience that can help us is that he realized that accepting her invitation would make him a thief, taking what belonged to another man. Joseph explained, "There is only one greater in this house than I, and he has withheld nothing from me except you, because you are his wife." If you are considering giving away your virginity—not knowing whether or not this is the person that you love enough and are committed to spend the rest of your life with—remember that the gift of yourself can be granted only once. There is only one "first time." Does that count for nothing?

In one more observation, Joseph realized that there is no sin in being tempted; rather, the sin lies in yielding to temptation. "How then," he asks her, "could I do such a wicked thing and sin against God?" (39:9).

"But Joseph," she could have said, "what does God have to do with us?" The incident which I have just related took place at least 400 years before the Ten Commandments were given, but Joseph knew there are moral laws which transcend the rise and fall of nations, the ebb and flow of social traditions and pop morality. We are responsible to God for our actions. Long ago, Paul wrote to a sexually permissive group of men and women and said,

> But remember this—the wrong desires that come into your life aren't anything new and different. Many others have faced exactly the same problems before you. And no temptation is irresistible. You can trust God to keep the temptation from becoming so strong that you can't stand up against it, for he has promised this and will do what he says. He will show you how to escape temptation's power so that you can bear up patiently against it. (1 Corinthians 10:13, TLB)

For a single living in a world of moral pollution, maintaining purity isn't easy, but it is possible. There are five guidelines I would like to share with you that will help you keep yourself pure.

Guideline #1: Run up your flag and commit yourself.

Nobody gets splashed with filth more than the person who is still floundering in the gutter. Head for higher ground and declare yourself. Run up your flag. This isn't a matter of thinking that you are holier than others but a matter of openly declaring yourself.

This first step is a combination of the prompting of the Holy Spirit within and your desire to be unstained with the sexual pollution of the world. James was talking about this very issue when he wrote that the kind of religion which God accepts includes "keep[ing] oneself from being polluted by the world" (James 1:27).

Guideline #2: Make a clean break with sexual sins.

Paul counseled, "count yourselves dead to sin but alive to God in Christ Jesus. Therefore do not let sin reign in your mortal body so that you obey its evil desires" (Romans 6:11-12). In the same letter he said we should "offer [our] bodies as living sacrifices, holy and pleasing to God" (Romans 12:1). But the problem with living sacrifices, so noted J. Vernon McGee years ago, is that they keep crawling off the altar. At times you have to reaffirm your commitment to sexual purity.

Guideline #3: Maintain purity by keeping a tidy house.

This business of maintaining sexual purity demands that there be confession and cleansing as you forsake what you know is wrong and hold fast to that which is right. This means renewal on a daily basis. It includes your thought life, your moral life and your business dealings. "If we confess our sins, he is faithful and just and will forgive us our sins and purify us from all unrighteousness," says First John 1:9. It still works today.

Guideline #4: Accept the discipline which comes from His hand.

There are times when you face the consequences of your wrong actions. You can pour out your heart to the Lord in earnest repentance, and God forgives you, but you still have to live with the consequences of what you did. A young man who took his father's car without permission was involved in an accident which was his fault. He stood by the front fender which had been badly damaged, closed his eyes and said, "Dear God, I pray that this did not happen!"

There are times when God allows difficulty which causes us to come to our senses and reverse the direction of our lives. It happened to the prodigal who "came to his senses" and decided it was time to go back to the father's house (Luke 15:17).

When you know that God has a loving heart, it is easier to accept the discipline which comes from His hand, causing your wayward steps to be reversed. Learn to know the difference between the touch of God's hand in gentle rebuke and the opposition of Satan, which must be resisted.

The most devastating day of my life came after three years of dating and I made the decision to propose to Darlene (who eventually became my wife). I knew that I loved her more than anything else in the world, and I wanted to spend the rest of my life with her. She said that she loved me (and I'm sure that she did). She was everything I wanted in a wife: a loving person, committed to the Lord, talented and beautiful and a great listener. I had just graduated from college and she had a year to go, so after much prayer and thought, I decided to propose with full anticipation that her acceptance was a done deal.

I bought the ring and drove from Denver to Laguna Beach, California where her family was vacationing. After a lovely dinner, we drove up on the bluffs overlooking the Pacific which was shimmering in moonlight. And then I popped the question.

She started crying and about all she could say was, "I can't. I'm not ready." I thought, *You've had three years to get ready. You knew this was coming. You love me. How can you say no?*

I was absolutely devastated. In the early hours of the morning, I picked up my Bible and began to read from Hebrews 12 which says, "My son, do not make light of the Lord's discipline, and do not lose heart when he rebukes you, because the Lord disciplines those he loves, and he punishes everyone he accepts as a son" (Hebrews 12:5-6).

Though I didn't learn about it for some time, that night Darlene turned at random to the book of Proverbs and read, "My son, do not despise the LORD's discipline and do not resent his rebuke, because the LORD disciplines those he loves, as a father the son he delights in" (Proverbs 3:11-12). Coincidence? No, part of the Lord's discipline in both of our lives.

We weren't ready for marriage. I thought we were communicating quite well, but she didn't think so.

Though she was a great listener, she wasn't really letting me in on what was going on in her head.

Our two families are very different. Mine are extroverts. If we think something, we say it. Her family, with a Canadian background, maintain a polite reserve. If they gave Olympic gold medals in nonverbal communication, surely her mother would have been a serious contender for one on the Canadian team. Her dad learned to read the nonverbal signals. Darlene's mother would sniff and her dad knew exactly what to do. But when Darlene sniffed, I gave her my handkerchief. I didn't understand she was trying to tell me something. I expected her to say it.

We didn't talk the same language, something we now know would seriously have hindered our relationship in marriage. So going nowhere in the relationship, we broke up, and though I still loved her, I dated other girls (usually maneuvering things so that her roommates would be sure to see us so they would give her a report that I wasn't sitting on my hands doing nothing!).

Then, after an uphill fight with lupus, a degenerative disease of the connective tissues, my sister died. Again I was devastated, and because Darlene knew my sister, we spent time together. I cried. She cried. And when she saw that I did have emotions and feelings and allowed her to see the real me— not just the outside veneer—our relationship changed quickly. And we learned how necessary it is to communicate and started communicating.

When God disciplines us, He is taking us into

the valley where we face difficulty which may be painful and certainly not to our choosing. Yet He hasn't abandoned us in the process. He's teaching us something we desperately need to learn. Sometimes we do sense that what has happened has been the result of our wrongdoing or wrong choices which are outside of the will of God, and we submit to His discipline knowing that it is the loving hand of the Father which brings us back into the path where He wants us to walk. At other times, we don't immediately understand, but later look back and recognize that what happened was discipline and we profited from it.

There are times when you, and others who are mature and godly, sense that God is definitely directing in something, and things just don't come together. That's when you need to apply a good dose of Ephesians 6 and trust God to work, turning around the circumstances. In those cases, it is Satan, not God who is opposing you.

Guideline #5: Encourage purity in a polluted world by practicing constant renewal.

Years ago the psalmist asked the question we face today: "How can a young man keep his way pure?" Then he answered his own question: "By living according to your word" (Psalm 119:9).

Renewal is a day-by-day matter. It is a matter of refocusing your life, of coming back to the foot of the cross and getting a new fix on what really counts. It begins every morning as your heart cries out, "Father, let's walk together today," and then you go back to the Word like a cleansing fountain to get a new glimpse of the eternal and a firm grip on the hand of the Almighty. I believe that three elements fit into this pattern of renewal:

- Be in the Word every day, applying biblical principles to your life, claiming verses which speak to your heart and finding direction and strength for living.

- Make prayer as natural a part of life as breathing, talking to the Lord freely about your concerns, your hopes and your ambitions, confessing failure and sin as necessary.

- Get involved in fellowship with other Christians. This can best be done through a local church where you belong and feel that you are part of a body.

This whole matter of maintaining purity is what the Bible describes as holiness. Striving for sexual purity is never easy and it's never final, but it's also never too late to begin its quest.

Choice #3: Commitment or nonbinding relationships?

When John and Marcia are together, their friends often introduce them as "Mr. and Mrs." People comment, "They seem married . . ." But the fact is, they have never been to the altar, and though Marcia talks about getting married (certainly before children come) and gets misty-eyed when her friends get married, there are no tangible plans for a wedding. John just isn't interested. "Marriage is too serious; it's scary," he says.

They are typical of a growing number of men and women who, for whatever reasons, choose to live together without getting married. Another co-habitating male explained, "I think living together lets us feel like we're still in our twenties. Being married means being an adult, [and] we still want to experience childhood." Who would question that marriage is an adult relationship, but since when has sleeping together become the prerogative of children? When asked why he didn't marry the girl he was living with, another male explained, "We just weren't into the whole wedding thing; we wanted to be 'together' rather than 'married,' and we still feel that way."

But not everyone plans on staying together. Take, for example, the young woman who wrote me: "I am a single woman who is going to have a baby outside of marriage. This is not to imply that we don't want to get married, but our feelings, especially those of the father of my baby, are still uncertain about a lifetime of commitment. But I love this new life in me so much that I was able to endure, through the Lord's strength, the criticism I have received from my parents and friends." I couldn't help but be reminded of a card which I saw recently. It pictured a couple in a warm embrace standing on the beach silhouetted by a beautiful sunset. The message read, "You are to me like the waves of the sea, holding me gently, leaving me free."

What's happened to commitment? A generation ago sexual privilege was accompanied by commitment. It was not an option; it was a given. Is it possible, as crude as the analogy is, that Elvis Presley gave us the answer? When he was asked about not getting married to the woman he was presently living with, he replied, "Why buy a cow when you can get milk through the fence?"

Commitment is a word that doesn't get a lot of press today, and when it does, it is often used in jest or humor. I'm thinking of the cartoon picturing a young man talking to his girlfriend. He says, "If you ever leave me, I'll have you committed." Being committed to someone or having him/her commit you is hardly the same thing. According to the dictionary, commitment is the act of giving or putting something in the trust of another. In the broader sense, it is the act of pledging or binding yourself to a certain course of action or to a person, as the case may be.

Commitment is the decision to go forward in a relationship, to hang in there when the going gets tough, to take one more step when you are convinced all strength is gone. In his book, *Whatever Happened to Commitment?* Ed Dayton observed:

> Commitment is at the foundation of all human relationships. It is the warp and woof of every society. No matter where

> we are in the world, the idea of commit-
> ment is well understood. It may work it-
> self out in different ways, but it is there.
> To be human is to long for commit-
> ments from others.[9]

Commitment is the decision to stand by someone no matter what the temperature of a relationship may be or the force of the wind that blows
against it.

Today, however, the attitudes of the world miti-
gate against commitment. "Do your own thing!
Seek your own fulfillment! Find satisfaction!" All
of these attitudes are viruses that destroy commitment. "We have become victims of liberation,"
says Arthur Fleming. He charges, "The life-style
philosophy of 'do your own thing' is a commitment to self. The attitude seems to be, 'I'm worth
it,' or 'I deserve it.' This kind of world is very
small. It contains only one person—self."

The question in the minds of a lot of women of
marriageable age is pretty basic: Why are men afraid
to make a commitment? Men are not the only ones
who hesitate to make a commitment. But by virtue
of the emotional framework which women have because of the way God made them, more women are
prone to make commitments to marriage than men.
They want someone who will stand by their side to
support, help and encourage them.

When I was counseling a young couple who
have now established a good marriage, I asked for
the story of how they met.

The young woman responded, "In a singles group at church." Then the young man began to tell how they had met three years earlier but after a short while he rather rudely broke off the relationship. Later they met again. He invited her to lunch and began by apologizing for the way he had treated her.

"Did you think this was a 'come on' or that he was sincere?"

"Oh, he was sincere," she commented, "but it took him a long, long time to get serious."

"I was afraid to make a commitment," he said.

"Do you mind telling me why?" I asked.

"My checklist was too high. Reality and fantasy were much too far apart. I kept thinking, *Maybe I will meet someone who is my perfect ten, who is more exciting than she is.*"

"What made you make the decision to commit?"

"I began to realize that fantasies or dreams are realized only in our thinking, that in the real world we all have imperfections. And besides, I realized that if I didn't make a commitment, I would lose her."

Many today, especially those who have grown up in dysfunctional families where there was little real happiness, are understandably hesitant to commit themselves to any relationship. They don't want the same thing to happen to them, and they think that by not making a commitment they can avoid unhappiness.

"Do you think George will marry the girl he's been dating?" I asked my son, referring to a mutual friend.

"No," Steve replied, explaining that as long as he has known George, he has been very serious about relationships, but he won't actually commit. George is coated with Teflon and nothing sticks.

Commitment goes far beyond relationships. No cause, no endeavor, no goal can really be attained without commitment. Some contend that today's youth are short on commitment, and with many that is true. But not all of them fall into that category. As a recreational cyclist, I tremendously admire the dedication and commitment of those who compete in serious biking competition, driving their bodies as they do. Take, for example, the Tour de France—one of the premier contests of biking—where day after day cyclists will maintain an average of thirty-five miles per hour (sixty km/h).

That takes commitment.

When Lindbergh flew the Atlantic for the first time, he took his map and drew a line at the halfway point. He made the decision that when he crossed that line, no matter what would happen, there would be no turning back; he would go on.

Perhaps one of the reasons we are so hesitant to make long-term commitments today is that we have not first committed ourselves to live as God has ordered. "When Jesus Christ calls a man," wrote Dietrich Bonhoeffer in a German prison cell shortly before his death, "He calls him to come and die." But death to our own desires, wishes and ambitions isn't a very pleasant thought. We want our strokes; we want our satisfaction.

In giving something through commitment, however, you gain far more than you give up. Take, for example, a Yugoslavian woman, born into a humble family, courted by poverty. When her brother, an army officer, chided her for committing her life to missionary service, she retorted, "You think you are so important as an officer, serving a king of 2 million subjects. Well, I am serving the King of the whole world. Which one of us is right?"

The brother was Lieutenant Bojaxhui. Ever heard of him?

His sister was known and loved around the world: Mother Theresa.

Her greatest reward, she often said, was not the Nobel Prize, given in recognition of those she helped, but the love of those she touched. Her commitment made the difference.

In this section I have told you how important commitment is in life when it comes to accomplishment—whether it is flying the Atlantic as Lindbergh did or establishing orphanages and hostels as Mother Theresa did. The same principle applies to relationships. Without that kind of unswerving, never-to-be-questioned commitment, a relationship cannot endure.

If you grew up in the kind of a home or environment where commitment with certainty was lacking, it won't be easy for you to incorporate this into your life. It begins with determination and is fortified by absolute honesty. Integrity is doing what you say you will do, and when you apply that to relationships, you are talking about commitment.

Choice #4: Significance or mediocrity

Scores of people define success only in terms of fame, fortune, power or achievement and miss the significance of making their lives count for more than accomplishment. Even though you may not like being reminded of this, you who are single are uncluttered by many of the responsibilities which encumber your married counterparts. That's why Paul stressed the fact that a single can do many things which he or she would never accomplish as a married. He explains that

> a married man is concerned about the affairs of this world—how he can please his wife—and his interests are divided. An unmarried woman or virgin is concerned about the Lord's affairs: Her aim is to be devoted to the Lord in both body and spirit. But a married woman is concerned about the affairs of this world—how she can please her husband. I am saying this for your own good, not to restrict you, but that you may live in a right way in undivided devotion to the Lord. (1 Corinthians 7:33-35)

Let me tell you about some of my heroes and heroines—single men and women, who chose the path of significance rather than of success in life.

William Borden—he turned his back on ease

Two wills were probated within a few days of each other in the spring of 1913. Both were handwritten. One was signed by the financier J. Pierpont Morgan; the other was signed by a twenty-five-year-old Princeton Seminary graduate, William Borden. Only weeks before, Borden had taken pen in hand—just in case anything should happen—and wrote his last will and testament as a slow-moving ship sailed to Egypt where he hoped to share the love of God with Muslims.

Both men were wealthy; both were believers in Jesus Christ. Borden was heir to a family fortune, and Morgan had spent his life building one of the world's largest financial empires. But when their wills were probated, it was discovered that Morgan, who died at age seventy-five, had left to Christian work less than half of what Borden had, though Borden died at one-third of Morgan's age. Morgan was successful; Borden was significant.

William Borden, however, left far more than a legacy of money when his life was cut short by cerebral meningitis. It wasn't Borden's money which impressed people; it was his life, his integrity, his thoughtfulness and his commitment to Jesus Christ. Born into a wealthy family, Borden could have had a life of leisure. Instead, he chose to become a missionary, serving in one of the world's most difficult places.

Converted as a teenager, Borden never let his money get in his way. In fact, people were often shocked to learn that this caring young man was actually quite wealthy. Borden never considered his money as belonging to him. He refused to buy a car, saying it was "an unjustified luxury." Even in Cairo, he rode oxcarts and lived with a local family.

During his seminary days he established a mission on skid row to reach alcoholics. At age twenty-three, he wrote what became the doctrinal charter for the Moody Bible Institute in Chicago. And when he died, newspapers around the world carried the story of this young man's untimely death. "What a waste of human potential!" cried so many. "Just think what he could have done with his life!"

William Borden would have agreed with what Paul wrote to the Philippians, saying that "Christ will be exalted in my body, whether by life or by death." Both he and Paul experienced the ultimate sacrifice. "For to me, to live is Christ and to die is gain" (Philippians 1:20-21).

Borden's life motto was "No reservation, no retreat, no regret." If, as the Westminster Confession of faith suggests, our chief end in life is to glorify God, William Borden did just that. He also demonstrated that it is not how long you live that counts, but how you live. He chose significance over affluence and comfort.

Amy Carmichael—she made a big difference

Amy Carmichael was a woman who didn't fit the

mold, a fact which resulted in a lot of problems for people who were more committed to order and tradition than to the teaching of God's Word. It wasn't that she was a rebel, but she was a non-conformist as a single in a couples' world. If you have never been introduced to Amy Carmichael, I highly recommend Elisabeth Elliot's book *A Chance to Die*. A former missionary herself who, as a single mother, went back to the tribe who had killed her husband, Elliot is quick to reveal her prejudice by placing Carmichael on a pedestal. Yet Elliot is candid in accurately portraying the humanity as well as the love in the life of this woman, who was one of the greatest of all missionaries in modern history.

Born on December 16, 1867, on the north coast of Ireland, Amy Carmichael was never destined for mediocrity. From her strict upbringing, Amy quickly learned that more was expected of her than of others. While other children were given peppermint candies to while away time in the long church services, the Carmichael children were expected to sit in quiet obedience.

In the early years of her missionary experience, Amy seemed to flounder. She first served in Japan, then China, then Ceylon and then back in England where no small amount of pressure was put on her to stay and serve. Finally the will of God took her to India, and there she spent the rest of her life. Among the many things that Amy Carmichael will be remembered for is her work among the children, especially the girls who were forced into temple prostitution. She became part of the work which had been established at Dohnavur, and that name eventually became synonymous with what she did.

Three words seem to characterize this great woman, who did what no man ever accomplished there: obedience, loyalty and tenderness. From the beginning there was fierce and unswerving obedience to the Word of God and what she felt was God's will for her life, something which traditional missionaries neither understood nor appreciated. In the early years of her work there was a "Get-Amy-Carmichael-out-of-India" movement among missionaries and other Indian Christians. "She was a thorn in their sides," writes Elisabeth Elliot, because she donned Indian saris and insisted on doing the work of a servant.

Out of obedience to the will of God came loyalty to those with whom she worked. She refused to speak against her critics and would not allow her co-workers to do so either. She insisted on absolute, unflagging loyalty to her brothers and sisters in Christ no matter how they appeared to be enemies of the work. In her book *Roots* she wrote, "It is not at all that we think that ours is the only way of living, but we are sure that it is the way meant for us." She did not believe that you could pray with and for someone and at the same time speak harshly of that person. She wrote, "But how can you pray—really pray, I mean—with one against whom you have a grudge or whom you have been discussing critically with another? Try it. You will find it cannot be done." Finally, through all she explained, tenderness marked this great woman's life.

At the age of eighty-four, on January 18, 1951, Amy slipped into the presence of the Lord after a long illness. Under a tamarind tree, in a grave marked only by the Indian word for mother, AMMAI, lies the remains of a woman who was as much a saint as any woman who ever lived. She refused to yield to the expectations of even her own family and society and accomplished what no male ever did in India.

Mary Slessor—a Scottish lass as tough as any lad

My third hero is a Scottish lass who in the 1840s was born into poverty in a home that was as barren as the nursery rhyme cupboard of Old Mother Hubbard. The decade was known as the "Hungry Forties," as crops failed and migrant workers were driven to the overcrowded, desolate cities. In 1848, Mary Mitchell Slessor was born to an alcoholic shoemaker whose wife was a weaver as well as the eventual mother of seven children. When drink finally overcame Robert, the scant wages of his wife caused the family to move to Dundee, where young Mary grew up. At the age of seven, she was forced to work in the mill half-time. This meant schooling had to fit in with the work schedule. Home was a tiny one-room flat with no water, no lighting and no sanitation facilities.

It was a tough world for this redheaded, streetwise young woman. She finally dropped out of school to work full time in the mill, but this girl who knew how to use her knuckles with the local rowdies retained a tender heart. When a missionary from the Calabar in Africa (now Nigeria) spoke in their local church, Mary's heart was inflamed. Everything, though, was against her becoming a missionary—everything and everybody but God. Nonetheless, God was able to use all of these circumstances in a mighty way to her advantage.

Many years later, Mary Slessor, who became known as Mary, Queen of the Calabar, wrote in her diary, "God plus one are always a majority—let me know Thou art with me." Mary Slessor—the fighting Scot from the slums of Dundee—went to an Africa which was reeling from the horrors of the slave trade. It was diseased by pagan customs, such as the killing of all twins because the natives were convinced that one had been fathered by the devil. Since they were uncertain as to which twin was so fathered, they immediately killed both.

The Africa to which Mary went was competing for the white man's money, weapons and booze. The impact of Mary Slessor, who sacrificed pleasure, health and almost her very life, is beautifully described in a book written by James Buchan entitled *The Expendable Mary Slessor*, which I recommend. Buchan describes Mary's accomplishments:

> She never opposed the African ways except where they degraded the Africans themselves. She had learned from St. Paul—"Paul laddie," she called him—

that her Lord loved these people enough to give His life for them, but loving them never meant acquiescing to the base aspects of pagan culture. She threatened and begged in order to save lives; she adopted dozens of African babies that were left to die in the bush. She fought for the right of the African women to be free from death at the whim of a man. For nearly forty years—until her death in 1915—she lived as an African, often in a village hut. When she died, thousands of Africans wept for the Eka Kpukpro Owo—Mother of all the peoples.[10]

She never married. Her work was her life. After many years in Africa, Mary returned to her native Scotland, a stooping, grey-haired woman, so wrinkled that people failed to recognize her while she was recuperating at the home of friends. Her hosts, the McCrindles, often heard her talking in her room. They thought the isolation and privation had actually affected her sanity, but upon listening to her conversation, they soon discovered that she was chatting with her Heavenly Father, a habit which Mary cultivated by keeping in constant touch with Him. If it is true that "when the going gets tough, the tough get going," then certainly that was true of the Scot whom I consider to be among the great Christian leaders of the last century—Mary Slessor, Queen of the Calabar.

That's only the beginning. Actually, I could write a book about singles and what they have accomplished. For example, there is Lillian Trasher, who went to Egypt and established orphanages. Lilian Dickson lived a pretty common life as the wife of a missionary and professor until her husband died, and then her life took a different direction. She established work for unmarried women, built churches for the lepers of Taiwan and stormed the world to challenge people to use what they have for God while literally standing on a soapbox because she was so short she couldn't see over the pulpit. Founder of an organization known as Mustard Seed, this woman accomplished far more as a single than she ever did as a married woman.

Most of the single individuals whom I really admire are women. Surprised? Perhaps the explanation is similar to that of David Ben Gurion who was asked about Golda Meier—why he backed her so singularly. He replied, "She's the best man I have in the cabinet." Possibly that's true of God's arsenal of real soldiers as well.

What Are Your Choices?

OK, what are the decisions you are forced to make in the near future? Dare to be different. Take the challenge. Go where you have never gone before. Do what you have always wanted to do but were afraid to try. Remember the trapeze artist has to let go of the bar he is holding and swing through space (scary!) before he catches the one on the other side of the set. You've got to be willing to let go of the familiar, the comfortable, the ordinary to accomplish the extraordinary. Whether you live a life of significance or mediocrity depends on your decisions. Go for it; you'll be glad you did.

Endnotes

1. *Orange County* [California] *Register*, June 14, 1990, Sec. A, p. 2.

2. Rick Steadman, *Pure Joy* (Chicago: Moody Press, 1993), p. 39.

3. Carolyn See, "The New Chastity," *Cosmopolitan*, November 1985, p. 83.

4. Mary Ann Mayo as quoted by Carolyn Koons and Micheal Anthony in *Single Adult Passages* (Grand Rapids, MI: Baker Book House, 1991), p. 137.

5. "The Revolution Is Over," *TIME*, April 9, 1984, p. 78.

6. "Sex with Care," *U.S. News and World Report*, June 1986, p. 53.

7. Ibid.

8. Joyce Brothers, *New World*, as quoted by Carolyn Koons and Michael Anthony, *Single Adult Passages*, pp. 138-139.

9. Ed Dayton, *Whatever Happened to Commitment?* (Grand Rapids, MI: Zondervan Books, 1984), p. 15.

10. James Buchan, *The Expendable Mary Slessor* (New York: Seabury Press, 1981), p. 254.

5

Handling OPE (Other People's Expectations)

*"I don't know the key to success, but the key to
failure is to try to please everybody."*

—Bill Cosby

"Have you been asked to marry?"

"Yes, several times."

"Really? I didn't know you had been that serious with anyone."

"Well, you see . . . I have been asked to marry someone several times—by my parents!"

Funny? Not when you are on the receiving end of the conversation.

Pressure to marry comes from parents, relatives, friends and society in general. If we were to invert a pyramid, I would put society on the top layer with parental pressure closest to you—underneath the pyramid.

It isn't difficult to understand from a historical perspective why society in general considers a single to be somewhat irregular. For centuries, singles—women, in particular—have been afforded a second-class place in society. Single men were considered to be less responsible than those who had married and assumed the responsibility of a family. Women found identity through a connection with a male. For example, Patricia as a child is Paul Smith's daughter, but at marriage she ceases to be Patricia Smith and becomes Mrs. John Brown—at least in most societies. Furthermore, throughout history, women, not being as strong as men physically, were considered to be in need of male protection by a father, brother or male family member until they married.

Until a generation ago, when young men and women graduated from high school and went on to further their education, it was assumed that by the time they finished they would have found a suitable prospective mate. Even in some Christian colleges where dating was not allowed, at graduation there would be a flurry of weddings, all of which were the result of long-distance relationships that had been nurtured through very discreet contact between the sexes.

For the girl who went through college and didn't find a mate, there were raised eyebrows and, more often than not, pointed questions or sarcasm. Society assumed that she was the "school marm type" (hair drawn back, thick glasses). The better educated and the more intelligent she was, the slimmer her chances of finding a husband, so popular wisdom decreed. This caused some parents to discourage graduate work. "Better to get a 'MRS.' degree than an M.A.," parents told their daughters. The primary goal of college was to find a suitable partner to marry, and when a girl faced her senior year without an engagement ring on her finger, "senior panic" set in.

Today things have changed considerably, but the layers of expectation are still very much with us. There is still a culturally induced pressure to marry and conform to the norm of living in a couples' world. Subsequently ninety-four percent of all females eventually marry. Out of this cultural expectation, three major misconceptions arise with which you who are single must cope:

- Something is wrong with the individual who is single.
- Individuals who are single are unhappy; therefore, married folks are doing them a favor to help them find suitable partners.
- A marriage which is less than ideal is better than facing life as a single.

Let's take a closer look at these one at a time.

Any individual who considers singleness to be defectiveness lacks both an understanding of human nature as well as a knowledge of Scripture. In giving us the book of Genesis, Moses noted that God recognized the intense loneliness of Adam. "It is not good for the man to be alone. I will make a helper suitable for him" (Genesis 2:18). When he had named the animals one by one, there was still none to whom Adam could relate as a peer. Is loneliness defectiveness? Needs and defects are not synonymous. God makes individuals unique, whole, complete. Yet Adam had a deep, intense longing for someone who could be a companion, a helper, a listener, a friend. Elijah, Daniel, Paul and even Jesus Christ were single most, if not all of their lives. Are they to be considered defective?

The second myth of the marrieds is that match-making comes with the high calling and special blessing of the Almighty. "He who finds a wife finds what is good," wrote the wise man Solomon long ago (Proverbs 18:22); therefore, helping singles find the "good thing" is to bestow them with great favor and blessing, right? Not according to

singles who resent matchmaking more than anything (with the possible exception of the "What's
the matter with you that you aren't married?" routine).

Others think that a marriage of convenience is
better than the best of single solitude. For better
or worse, marriage only compounds problems and
situations. One woman who attended a conference
at which I spoke fully realized that fact. At the end
of the conference individuals were invited to share
what God had impressed upon their lives. She
stood and said. "I'm fifty years old and single and
glad of it. The thrill of what I have missed has
been swallowed up by the joy of what I have been
spared." Among those who laughed the loudest
were those who hurt the most.

OK, you are a single living in a couples' world.
Like it or not (and you probably don't), you aren't
going to change the way your mother sighs, wishing you could "meet a nice boy" or the way your
dad critiques the friends you bring home, asking
about their income, family connections and education. They are parents, and that's the way it is.

Remember, you can't control the circumstances
or the attitudes of other people. But you *can*
choose your response to them.

What Are Your Options?

- anger
- tell them it is none of their business
- advise them to "get out of your face"

- play games
- go along with the "let's pretend" scenario, letting them think that you are out there looking over the field from every possible perspective, checking out everything that comes down the street
- be your own person with resolute independence, putting a wall between you and OPE
- or what?

Before I give you some thoughts about how to fight back, I'd like you to take a look at your own attitude. Would you say that hostility toward OPE is driving a wedge between you and people who really love you, who in spite of their clutsiness really care about you? Is it also possible that the pressures of OPE seem to put some distance between you and God? You know how you feel after you have prayed for a mate and nothing happens. You become convinced that either you are doing something wrong, you are not good enough or else God has the switch turned off on the amplifier and doesn't hear your prayer.

Do you ever take time to consider your life from God's vantage point? Do you ever think about the fact that He may have something on the horizon so special that if you saw it, you would rejoice that you had patience enough to await His timing? How would He have you respond to the pressures you feel?

Take a few moments and pencil in the way you feel.

Getting OPE Out in the Open

	Their expectations	My attitude toward them
Parents		
Relatives		
Friends		
Society		
What God expects from me		

Got it done? Good. In light of what you have just written, consider the following guidelines which will help you cope with OPE. I guarantee that they can make a difference in the way you respond to the uncomfortable expectations of others.

Guideline #1: Refuse to accept responsibility for your failure to meet OPE.

Few people discover the intensity of their inner strength until they are required to stand alone without the support to which they have grown accustomed. As long as someone lets us lean on him or her, we take the path of least resistance and draw strength from that person, whether it be a parent or a best friend. When you are forced to stand emotionally on your own, you begin to walk, much like a baby. You may have some bumps and tumbles, but you'll make it.

This is not to suggest that you purposefully create barriers between yourself and those who have great expectations for you. On the contrary, work to keep the lines of communication open. Just don't let others put you under a guilt trip because you can't measure up. After all, sending the clouds scurrying and bringing the sunshine isn't within your control.

Guideline #2: Stop worrying about the future.

In her book *Each New Day*, Corrie ten Boom, a single woman who grew up in a couples' world, a woman who probably knew more pressure than you could ever possibly know in your lifetime, wrote, "When I worry, I go to the mirror and say to myself, 'This tremendous thing which is worrying me is beyond a solution. It is especially too hard for Jesus Christ to handle.' After I have said that, I smile and I am ashamed."

Right now make a list of what you are worried about (including not finding the right person to marry). Write down everything you can think of.

Go back over the list and put an X beside the issues which really bother you, which you feel are too big for God to help you with. Come on, be honest.

Then ask yourself, "Are these issues hindering my growth as a person?" Now, how do we deal with the sin of worry, which is a greater problem than OPE?

The Bible tells you what to do. It says, "Cast all your anxiety on him because he cares for you" (1 Peter 5:7). Psalm 55:22 has similar words of advice, "Cast your cares on the LORD and he will sustain you." I like the way Ken Taylor translated Philippians 4:6: "Don't worry about anything; instead, pray about everything; tell God your needs and don't forget to thank him for his answers" (TLB).

Putting God's psychiatry into practice means you have to do what C.S. Lewis advised: Tell your emotions where to get off. It means you've got to make the conscious decision that you are going to trust God for a solution to your worries (letting Him meet the need His way, not yours). You've got to let Him take the night shift, meaning you in effect say, "Lord, this is too big for me. It isn't necessary for both of us to stay awake worrying about this tonight. You take over, and help me know how to respond to the expectations of _____."

Thomas Bair once wrote, "It is God's will that I should cast my care on Him each day (1 Peter 5). He also asks me not to cast my confidence [in Him] away (Hebrews 10). But, oh, how stupidly I act when taken unaware; I cast away my confidence, and carry all my care." Agree?

Today is the tomorrow that you worried about yesterday! Live for today and make this day an airtight twenty-four-hour module where you find God's grace and strength. When you get up, say, "Lord, let's walk together just today! I want to live this day to the fullest and not let worry about tomorrow rob me of the joy of being alive today." That attitude can make a difference.

Guideline #3: Start making choices which are in line with what God wants you want to do.

There are three kinds of singles in the world:

- Accusers
- Excusers
- Choosers

The *accusers* are the ones who want to blame others for their circumstances. "I'd be happily married today, if Agatha hadn't married the postman when I was working in Saudi. (I promised to write every day and did.)" The accuser says, "It's not my fault." Rick Warren asks, "Who are you blaming for your unhappiness? You spell 'blame' B-LAME. Whenever you are blaming someone else, you are 'being lame.' "

The *excusers* are the ones who have an alibi for their problems. "If I were only prettier, I'd attract someone." "If I just weren't overweight." "If I had money like . . ."

If you are looking for an excuse, you will come up with one. Accepting responsibility for your life is the first step toward being in control, instead of responding to OPE and trying to live up to the hopes of others, parents included.

The *choosers* are the ones who make things happen. They are the ones who are in control. The greatest power that God gave you is the power of determination—deciding which way you are going with your life and making the decision to act, not react to the circumstances of life.

Guideline #4: Set some goals for your life which are attainable and then break them down into one-step-at-a-time modules.

Someone suggested that smart goals have the following elements:

S—specific
M—motivational
A—attainable
R—relevant
T—tractable

Goals that are ambiguous, beyond your reach, impractical or unclearly defined are worse than none at all. Some say shoot at the moon, and if you miss it you'll end up in the stars. I disagree. Shoot at the moon and you're liable to end up in outer space. You may even need help getting back to earth. Only five percent of all singles have any real goals for their lives (apart from getting married or becoming wealthy enough to retire by age thirty-five), which may explain why only five percent of all individuals ever rise above the level of mediocrity.

What are your goals?

__ Go back to school and finish your degree.

__ Learn how to use a computer.
__ Get a job.
__ Join a singles group at church.
__ Volunteer to tutor kids.
__ Work in the nursery.
__ Take a summer ministry trip.
__ Join a health club.
__ Learn a hobby.

Think about *life goals* as well. Luke 2:52 says that "Jesus grew in wisdom and stature, and in favor with God and men." In this statement I see four goals which should serve as a model for what you want to see happen in your life:

1. Acquire wisdom—not simply knowledge—in life.
2. Attain physical growth (get in shape).
3. Spiritual growth.
4. Social development.

Guideline #5: Practice daily random acts of kindness and give love to someone who is not very lovable.

When you are doing combat with OPE, you get defensive—you raise the drawbridge of life, put up the defenses and retreat into the castle of your own thoughts. You need to reverse this mentality. Take the offensive. Do something positive. Going out of your way to dispense kindness and love is one of the greatest antidotes to the "poor me" mentality you will ever find.

Put some flowers on the desks of co-workers, take your grandmother for lunch, find a boy who has no dad and take him fishing or to a ball game. In simple terms, get out of the "me" mode and into the "giving of myself" mode. It's amazing how this will be a mood elevator for you, and at the same time you will touch someone's life for good and for God.

Guideline #6: Start being honest all of the time.

You don't have to handle OPE by being compliant (otherwise known as knuckling under to their expectations). You don't have to do everything that people would like you to do (including meeting all the cousins, friends, relatives, etc., of your aunt or godmother).

You may say, "But I don't want to hurt anybody!"

Don't you count for anything?

We often wear masks to hide the feelings we have because we don't have the courage to be honest. God hates hypocrisy and deceit, even though it may be well intended. It's OK to say (though I would try to do it as kindly as possible), "Look, I'm just not comfortable with the thought of coming to the Christmas dinner by myself when I'm the only single there among couples. Tell you what—how about having lunch with me and I can catch up on what's happening in your life. I really do want to know, but I'm through trying to fake situations which make me feel like a fifth wheel."

How honest are you with people? Which of the following best describes you?

___ I hesitate to be completely open and honest with people because I don't want to hurt them.

___ I tell people as much as I think they can handle and then shut down.

___ I avoid situations which make me uncomfortable though I will not honestly tell people why.

___ I've learned to be honest—completely—but I am willing both to sustain and inflict some discomfort if necessary.

It is at this point that you have to separate cultural expectations from what God would have you do, which is in your own best interest. *How* you do things can make a lot of difference, but you need to stop playing games when it comes to how you feel as a single in a couples' world and make the decision that is best for you.

Guideline #7: Break out of the routine.

Choose to create new options in your life by saying at least once a day, "I will consciously break out of the bondage of OPE and do something which is entirely my choice and decision." Break out of the mold you grew up with, the mold of relatives', friends' and associates' expectations. I'm not suggesting that you do something daring or bold, something immoral or racy, something which violates your conscience and your sense of worth, but instead do *something which is strictly out of the ordinary routine for your life.* Like what? Consider the following and add your thoughts to the end of the list.

- Start a hobby.
- Go to the nearest hospital and sign up as a volunteer.
- Take piano, voice, drum or guitar lessons.
- Take a child to the circus.
- Go on a missions tour somewhere.
- Volunteer to give your Christmas day working at an orphanage or cooking dinner for homeless people.
- Stop at a coffeehouse on the way home from work and treat yourself.
- Buy yourself a new dress, jacket or shirt (provided you have the money to pay for it).
- Take flying lessons or skydive out of an airplane.
- Learn to snorkel.
- Find someone who is hurting and listen.
- Take a CPR class. (You may need to revive some shocked people!)

Guideline #8: Reach out and help a hurting person.

One of the reflexes we have is to withdraw when we have been rejected, when our love has been unrequited or when we have suffered disappointment. But when you reach to help another, you help yourself.

When a war correspondent in the Korean War

picked up an orphaned child and took him to a nearby orphanage, one of the sisters told Bob Pearce, "We can't take him." She explained that at least four people were eating out of every rice bowl. Bob remonstrated, "Surely, you can take just one more child."

The sister picked up the orphaned child, carried him over and deposited the child in his lap and said, "Here. Now what will you do with him?"

Bob did what you would do. He reached in his pocket and gave the little money he had to buy rice. Then he returned to his home in the U.S. and began to raise money for children. That incident led to his establishing World Vision, an organization which subsequently has helped millions of people.

One of the myths which you have to overcome to live a life of significance and purpose is the mistaken belief that you don't count, that you can't make a difference in the world, that what you can do is so insignificant and the needs of the world are so great that what you can do doesn't matter.

It matters tremendously to someone who is on the receiving end of your love. For that one, it matters.

Guideline #9: Be a friend to someone who is friendless.

Extending friendship to those who need it is necessary. You must stop looking at other people with the same expectations and frame of reference which you so detest (for instance, that only beautiful people are worth befriending!). People with emotional scars, people who are overweight, people of a different race or faith, perhaps with "different" personalities (possibly the result of feeling badly about themselves), people who are shy or insecure—*all are worth getting to know!* They, too, are made in the image of God. In befriending someone, you yourself gain.

Guideline #10: Bring your pain and frustration with OPE to the Lord.

David experienced rejection, failure, broken relationships and intense pain. He was the youngest of eight, often passed over, considered to be somewhat of an outcast who took care of his father's sheep. He cried out, "Though my father and mother forsake me, the Lord will receive me" (Psalm 27:10). He wrote, "From the end of the earth will I cry unto thee, when my heart is overwhelmed: lead me to the rock that is higher than I" (Psalm 61:2, KJV).

Have you learned that there is One to whom you can turn, who understands, who knows the feelings of hostility, hurt and anger, the smart of rejection and the loneliness of your pain? His name is Jesus Christ, and you can trust Him.

God's help enables you to overcome what you cannot handle on your own. His will and purpose for your life are for your own good—the topic of chapter 7.

6

Can't We Just Be Friends?

"There are 'friends' who pretend to be friends,
but there is a friend
who sticks closer than a brother."

(Proverbs 18:24, TLB)

The questionnaire was addressed to "The Single Occupant." Obviously it was intended for my son. Among the questions certain to get a rise from any single were the following:

- Are you in a dead-end relationship or in a relationship of convenience?
- Have you been meeting people who in the beginning seem to have everything you want and then you discover they are totally different people?
- Are you frustrated by the games you have to play to meet someone special?
- Are you tired of the wrong men always approaching you, so that you have to keep saying, "No, thank you," while the man you would like to meet never approaches you?
- Are you uncomfortable about what to say to a woman when you first meet, hoping she doesn't think it is a pick-up line?

There is one thing for certain: Relationships are important. But in many cases, reaching out to someone as a person, as a friend, is interpreted as a sexual invitation—something you never intended. Question: Is it possible to establish non-romantic friendships with members of the opposite sex? Must all of your *real* friends be of the same gender as you? In dealing with this subject, let's first take a look at what friendship is about and then go on to gender specifics.

In his book *Quality Friendship*, Gary Inrig tells about two friends who both enlisted in the military, were sent overseas together and fought alongside each other. During an enemy attack, one of the men was critically wounded and was unable to crawl back to the safety of the foxhole. The friend lay dying in the no-man's land created by the crossfire of the two opposing sides.

Hearing the cries of his wounded buddy, the soldier decided to try to rescue his friend, but the sergeant in charge yelled, "It's too late. You can't do him any good, and you'll only get yourself killed." Realizing that it was almost suicidal to try, the man nonetheless started crawling toward his friend.

He reached him, too. Then a few minutes later, half-crawling, half-staggering back, he made it back to the foxhole with his friend cradled in his arms— dead. But in rescuing his friend, the soldier had also taken several hits and now he himself was dying.

The sergeant was both angry and moved with emotion as he cried, "What a waste. He's dead and you're dying. It just wasn't worth it." Gasping for breath, the soldier cried, "Oh, yes, it was, Sarge. When I got to him, the only thing he said was, 'I knew you'd come, Jim!' "[1]

What could better illustrate the truth of what Jesus said: "Greater love has no one than this, that he lay down his life for his friends" (John 15:13)? Have you made the discovery that you have lots of acquaintances in life and some who want to be known as your friends—especially when you have money or throw parties with good food—but there are few individuals who are real friends, the kind that would risk his or her life for you, the kind that would go to the wall with you no matter what you have done, no matter what happens?

Actually, there are three levels of friendship. The first level can be described as casual friends, more accurately described as acquaintances. Calling them friends is, of course, accommodating and gracious on your part. But if you dropped off the end of the pier somewhere, it would take a considerable length of time for them to find out about your disaster unless they read about it in the newspaper. Few tears would be shed. In all probability they wouldn't bother to attend your funeral even if they learned what had happened to you.

The second level of friends consists of the ones that you meet socially—in church, at parties, on the job, etc. When your name comes up, they identify with you as a friend. These friends, however, would also disappear very quickly if your company went broke, your name appeared in the paper in conjunction with a plot to overthrow the local school board or you got caught trying to steal the crown jewels. When your name came up, they are the ones who would say, "You know, I never was sure about that guy/girl. There was always something a little shady about him/her."

Psychologist Rollo May believes that most people make 500 to 2,500 acquaintances every year—

people you work with, individuals whom you meet at church or school or acquaintances with whom you share an elevator every work day or who live in the same apartment complex. The checker at the grocery store, the gas station attendant, your mailman or doctor—you nod or wave politely when you meet these folks, but by no stretch of the imagination could most acquaintances be considered real friends, the kind that would stand with you no matter what happens. But of that large number Dr. May believes that, on an average, only seven are *real friends*.[2]

That brings us to the third level of friendship which consists of only a few people. These are *real* friends—intimate friends, if you will. They are the ones who will stand with you no matter what you do, no matter what you look like, no matter whether you are up or down. They're there, and you can count on them for sure.

For just a minute stop and take time to count the number of real friends that you have—the ones who are absolutely committed to you no matter what might happen.

List five people who you would consider to be this kind of a friend:

1.
2.
3.
4.
5.

If you filled in every line you are blessed, and should you have ten such quality friends, you should shout with joy. As the writer of Proverbs put it 3,000 years ago, "There are 'friends' who pretend to be friends, but there is a friend who sticks closer than a brother" (Proverbs 18:24, TLB). You can never have too many of these friends. Now go back and circle those who are the same sex as yourself. Any left without a circle?

What Is a Friend?

Today a travel agent whom I have never met was talking to me about travel plans, and he kept saying, "Look, I'm telling you this as a friend. You really are my friend, you know!" I don't even know the man. He is probably a very fine gentleman, but for all I know, he may be an escapee from a mental institution or have a police record.

What is a friend? An Arab proverb answers the question: "A friend is one to whom we may pour out the contents of our hearts, chaff and grain together, know that the gentlest of hands will sift it, keep what is worth keeping, and with a breath of kindness blow the rest away!"[3] Not bad.

Many of the letters which come to us at *Guidelines* tell of strained or broken relationships. I'm thinking of the rather plaintive letter which came from a young man whose marriage had failed, who seemed to have problems getting along with people at work, and who finally wrote, "I would give almost anything for just one real friend!" Can you relate to that?

I suspect, however, that he was waiting for someone to bequeath friendship upon him much like an inheritance which comes from an unknown benefactor. Those things just don't happen. Like anything else that is really valuable, friendships take work as well as risk.

Friendship begins as you reach out to someone else. Proverbs 18:24 says, "A man that hath friends must show himself friendly" (KJV). Could that be your problem? General George Patton was a man of great talents, but he had very few friends. One of his biographers says of him, "He gained the generalship, the medals, and the glory, but he was never to make any friends."[4] Strange, isn't it, that someone who was such a leader ended up being respected but not considered a real friend to anyone?

An individual who is aloof and separate doesn't have many friends. You don't intend to be like that, yet folks consider you to be rather cold and "standoffish." Possibly you want friends, but it seems you end up without them. You withdraw—not because you are afraid to get down on the level of the playing field—but because you feel inadequate or insecure, and you are afraid of being rejected.

Somewhere there is a person who shares your interests, your thoughts and ideas and is hurting for a friend as badly as you are. There is a strange thing about friendship: Two individuals may be from different social backgrounds, different generations and even different cultures, yet they are drawn together in friendship that spans the differences.

Being vulnerable with each other, an essential of real friendship, means that you must lower the drawbridge across the moat of loneliness which separates you from the crowd. Opening the door allows someone to enter into your life. Try to remember that the world is not filled with strangers, only people who are searching for a real friend.

The Glue of Friendship

Truth is always stranger than fiction. Take, for example, the strange friendship of two young men who should have been bitter enemies. Instead, they became the closest of friends. One was raised in the palace of a king and knew the luxuries which are associated with that social status. The other was an uneducated youth who rose from obscurity and threatened to usurp the throne. Their names: David and Jonathan.

You can read about them in the Old Testament book of First Samuel. Of David, Gary Inrig writes, "David was ignored by his father and disliked by his brothers. He was the runt of the litter, who lived with the bitterness of rejection and neglect."[5] In spite of this, David had a relationship with the Lord which sustained him in his darkest hours. He is the one who wrote, "The LORD is my shepherd" (Psalm

23:1). He also said, "Though my father and mother forsake me, the LORD will receive me" (27:10).

These two met following David's great victory over the giant Goliath. After David had been presented to Jonathan's father, the king, the young prince Jonathan stayed behind to talk to David. Here's the record:

> After King Saul had finished his conversation with David, David met Jonathan, the king's son, and there was an immediate bond of love between them. Jonathan swore to be his blood brother, and sealed the pact by giving him his robe, sword, bow, and belt. (1 Samuel 18:1-4, TLB)

The New American Standard Bible put it, "The soul of Jonathan was knit to the soul of David, and Jonathan loved him as himself" (18:1). What bonding! They had every reason to be enemies, yet became friends.

In the strange but powerful attraction of these two men, a pattern emerges which gives us insights to help us understand what real friendship is all about.

In this friendship I see a number of elements. First, there was *absolute loyalty*. Jonathan could have betrayed his friend and eliminated him as a contender for the throne. Instead, in the words of Scripture, "he loved him as himself." Instead of betraying him, he protected him, endangering his own life in the process. "Whatever you want me to do, I'll do for you," Jonathan told David (20:4). See if you get that response the next time you ask a friend to come over and help you paint your house.

Second, *each accepted the other "as is,"* without trying to make the other into something he was not. They were nonjudgmental, something which is absolutely necessary for friends to stay friends. Jonathan never tried to improve David's manners or dress. When the women danced in the streets and sang, "Saul has slain his thousands, and David his tens of thousands" (18:7), out of jealousy King Saul became angry, but Jonathan defended his friend.

Another ingredient of real friendship is *absolute trust.* When things got very uncomfortable as Saul tried to kill David, the two made a pact, a covenant, and David pledged his honor to protect and honor Jonathan's descendants forever—something which he later did. Jonathan, in turn, found out the king's intentions and passed that information on to David, who fled for his life. Samuel describes this, "And Jonathan had David reaffirm his oath out of love for him, because he loved him as he loved himself" (20:17). What commitment!

Another element which is often lacking in friendships today is the *determination* of these two men to listen to each other, to encourage each other and to help each other no matter what the personal cost.

When a friend of mine encountered some difficulties in his personal life, he laid plans to take his life, to make it appear to be an accident so his wife could collect insurance. In the process, he came to himself, thinking, *This is not what I want to do with my life!* and he turned to me for help.

By profession the man is an attorney, and a very good one. He can argue very persuasively that purple looks green on a cloudy day, and that there are some very good things about chain saw murderers. He's convincing, too.

He's smarter than I am, so there was no sense in trying to convince him that his plan was rather foolish. Besides, he knew all of this. There was one thing that I could provide as a friend which he desperately needed. I could listen without passing judgment, without commenting. I could hurt for him. I could cry with him. And that is what I did.

We began meeting together once a week for breakfast, and I listened and listened. Gradually, he began to get a new grip on God and on his personal life. About then the neighbor who lived across the street from him encountered financial problems and was about to lose his home.

"Could I meet with you?" he asked, so the twosome became a threesome. Eventually the numbers grew, and over a period of several years a considerable number of men came, shared their deepest problems and reached out for help. Out of this intense need, friendships began to develop.

We asked three things of each other—all of which David and Jonathan incorporated into their friendship:

1. Keep each other's confidence absolutely.
2. Pray earnestly for each other.
3. Use what skills you have to help each other.

The writer of Proverbs tells us that "a friend loves at all times" (Proverbs 17:17), and never was that more true in than the relationship of David and Jonathan. In our "what's in it for me?" world today, have we lost sight of what true friendship is about? Have we begun to consider people as "assets" who can move us forward in our career or help us get to where we want to go? Of course, we all recognize that is taking place today. Yet you may be amazed at the number of men and women who will respond to the kind of commitment I've just described. People are starving for relationships which are deep enough and strong enough to bear each other's burdens.

One more element of friendship should be mentioned which connected David and Jonathan: *common interests*. David and Jonathan had a great deal in common, such as their ages, their interests in the welfare of the nation, their faith in God, their commitment to integrity and honesty, and a great deal more. Generally friends share interests in common—sports, work, church or something—but that is not always what brings people together. Sometimes individuals who have very diverse interests become very close friends—say, a youth and an elderly person or two people from different cultures or backgrounds. When that happens, it is relationship, not simply hobbies or interests, which brings them together.

Was David's Friendship with Jonathan "More Than Just Friendship"?

In our culture we have developed such a jaded sense of sexuality that some allege that Jonathan and David were homosexual lovers. There is not one shred of biblical or secular evidence to support such a charge, and based upon the culture of the day, the very thought is without foundation, as well as abhorrent. The law of Moses strictly forbade homosexuality, and furthermore, as Gary Inrig put it, "David could not be called the man after God's own heart if he was engaged in a sin the Bible so directly condemns, nor could it be said that 'the LORD was with him' (1 Samuel 18:14)."[6]

Putting that issue aside, let's go one step further as we look at different kinds of friendship.

Can't We Just Be Friends?

"Dear Dr. Sala," wrote a friend of *Guidelines,* "Every time I try to befriend someone of the opposite sex, that person interprets my friendship as a romantic gesture. This really bothers me, and it is not my intention. Can't we just be friends?"

If you were answering that question, what would you say? It's easy to say the problem is that men and women don't read signals the same way. What you intend as an expression of Christian friendship, others interpret as a come on. Then you end up *losing* a friend when you have to say, "Whoa! Can't we just be friends?"

In the first century there was a marked separation between the world of the sexes. A woman generally didn't appear in public apart from the company of her husband, and there wasn't a lot of social intercourse between men and women as friends. That, of course, was part of the culture. Yet as you read the New Testament, you understand that Jesus was a friend to many women—Mary, Martha, Mary Magdalene, the woman at the well of Sychar and many others. Women ministered to His needs wherever He traveled, yet there is not the faintest hint that His friendship was interpreted as anything but a gesture of sincere love.

Writing to a young man who was the pastor of a church, Paul gave us some guidelines as to how to develop nonsexual friendships. He said, "Treat younger men as brothers, older women as mothers, and younger women as sisters, with absolute purity" (1 Timothy 5:1-2). Here's how this translates into life today.

Guideline #1: Be genuine and sincere with members of the opposite sex.

Get across the message, "I care about you as a person, but my interest is in you as a human being, not as a sexual object or a possible mate." Our English word *sincere* comes from two Latin words *sin* and *cere* meaning "without wax." In Roman days when builders vied with each other for the lucrative contracts to build mansions, if some craftsmen without scruples would carelessly chip or crack a piece of granite which was going into a home or monument, they would conceal the crack with wax instead of replacing the piece with a perfect one.

They got away with the wrongdoing until the warm Italian sun melted the wax and the flaw was discovered; hence, a clause was inserted into most contracts, saying that the work was to be done *sin cere,* "without wax."

Being sincere with someone means that you are open. You accept someone for what he or she is— neither more nor less. Your integrity is not flawed. You have no hidden agenda.

Guideline #2: Be careful not to send conflicting signals.

Joe was a junior in college and during the summer when he was home, he dated a girl in his church a couple of times—just for fun, nothing more than that. But when he got back to school, he learned that she had enrolled at his school. Wanting to help her get acquainted and established, he went out of his way to show her around and introduce her to his friends—something she interpreted as an indication that he was more than just friendly.

He wasn't. When word got back to Joe that his friend probably wouldn't have gone to the same school had she known that he wasn't interested in her, he was dumbfounded. Though the two had been good friends, the situation became awkward and strained. Finally he had to confront her and tell her that he liked her as a friend and nothing more.

Be careful not to send conflicting signals. Sometimes gestures of friendship are misinterpreted. Don't lead someone to believe that you have more than friendly interest.

Many women tend to read more into the situation than is really there. If his is more than a friendly interest, that will be obvious as time goes on. In the meanwhile remember that a solid friendship is the foundation upon which a more serious relationship can be built.

Guideline #3: Realize a real friend complements someone without smothering that person.

A person may be so desperate for a friend that when someone does reach out in genuine friendship, the other person latches on to him or her the way a drowning person clings to a lifeguard. The other can't take it. Respect the space of the other person without suffocating that person. Simply put: Don't expect to be the only friend the other has. Give room to keep other friendships as well.

Guideline #4: Take a sincere interest in others.

Frankly, everybody loves to talk about himself or herself. A few lead questions like, "Tell me about yourself. We've worked together for several months, but I really don't know much about you," may well open the door for better understanding. You can appreciate someone's problems much better if you know where the person is coming from.

Guideline #5: Focus on group interaction as opposed to one-on-one encounters.

Lunch as a threesome doesn't send the same signal as spending time as a twosome. Including friends socially as well as someone special doesn't bring the relationship into a one-on-one focus, and it also allows you a greater degree of comfort getting acquainted.

Guideline #6: Follow through on your commitments as a friend.

Be someone who can be counted on, who keeps confidence, who is honest and who knows when to speak and when to remain silent.

Safeguarding Friendship

Is there such a thing as a platonic friendship—one without sexual motivation with a member of the opposite sex? Can you just be friends with a person and put the whole gender issue aside? Yes, and you can enrich your life by having friends of the opposite sex.

But how do you keep friendships from becoming romances which you neither welcome nor encourage? If you question whether a friendship is pushing the limits of what you consider to be appropriate, ask yourself the following questions:

Question #1: Is my friendship without ambition? Do I really care about this person as a friend, or do I have a romantic interest in this person? Men, by virtue of the fact that they are much more visually oriented and physically attracted than women, are more prone to establish a friendship with a person, then be attracted to the same person sexually in such a manner that goes beyond friendship.

Question #2: Does my friendship enrich the lives of all who are concerned? This means you need to look at the circumstances of a friendship. There are times when friendships become unequal relationships, and the one whom you consider to be a friend is constantly dumping on you. You feel like you are trying to swim and support a drowning person and you don't have the strength to handle it. The end result is that you feel used and worn. Telling your friend this brings the risk of misunderstanding, because being a real friend does involve being there to provide a listening ear. But a one-way friendship may be more than you can handle.

Question #3: Am I willing, so my friendship doesn't turn into romantic involvement, to avoid being alone in a situation which would lend itself to temptation which I might not be able to handle? This may mean saying no to business trips which pair you with the friend. It may mean you work alone finishing that report instead of working together on it after hours.

Hey, you may be thinking, *isn't that going a bit overboard?* Not if your frame of reference is what Paul wrote when he said, "Avoid every kind of evil" (1 Thessalonians 5:22), and the King James Version refers to avoiding even the "appearance of evil."

Here are several guidelines which will help you preserve the friendship you feel is important.

Guideline #1: Make it clear that you value your friendship for the sake of friendship.

This means you avoid flirting or sending sexual messages that say, "Come closer to me; I'm lonely." You may also need to let someone know that interest in you beyond friendship is sexual harassment and is both unwanted and threatening to your friendship.

Guideline #2: Dress appropriately.

If you question what message your appearance sends, ask a sibling or a friend of the opposite sex. What you consider to be stylish may be an open solicitation for the kind of attention which you don't want.

Guideline #3: Know when to say "no!"

If a friendship goes beyond the bounds of what you consider appropriate and you have no intention of getting involved romantically, politely remove someone's hand from your body and confront the issue. Surprising as this may seem to you, knowing when to say "Whoa" often preserves a friendship instead of allowing it to deteriorate. When someone really is a friend, that person respects your desires and standards.

Guideline #4: Follow the guidelines of Scripture: Treat older women as mothers, younger women as sisters, young men as brothers, older men as fathers.

Sexual harassment wouldn't exist if men followed the guidelines which Paul gave to Timothy long ago. This means that there can be warm friendship without familiarity. Because of the highly charged atmosphere around simple contact today, you can't be too careful.

Guideline #5: Communicate openly and honestly.

Some individuals would rather roll on a bed of ground glass than confront someone. They are the ones who run and hide when they feel threatened. It is much better to address issues directly which are of concern to you. When you are bothered by something, you can control the time, the place and the manner of confrontation.

Instead of saying, "You . . . ," it is much better to describe your feelings, saying something like, "I'd like you to know how I feel when . . ." and you address the issue as Jesus said we must (see Matthew 18:15). Another means of dealing with situations when you feel that a friendship is threatened is to say something like, "I've got a problem and I need your help in solving it. I value your friendship as a person, but I feel like it's moving beyond the level of friendship, and I'm not ready for this. Can you help me?"

Guideline #6: *If improprieties develop, don't let the issue go unchallenged.*

To protect yourself in the workplace, as embarrassing as it may be, report wrongdoing to your superior. Such tough love may be the only thing that will work in helping someone understand how to keep a friend a friend.

A real friend is a priceless gift which needs to be preserved. But when someone goes beyond the limits of propriety, you not only lose your respect for the friend, you lose a friend as well.

Endnotes

1. Gary Inrig, *Quality Friendships* (Chicago: Moody Press, 1981), p. 71.

2. As quoted by Jerry and Mary White, *Friends & Friendship* (Colorado Springs, CO: Navpress, 1982), p. 33.

3. As quoted by Walter Knight, *Master Book of Illustrations* (Grand Rapids, MI: William B. Eerdmans Publishing Co., 1956), p. 237.

4. As quoted in Muriel James and Louis Savary, *The Heart of Friendship* (San Francisco: Harper and Row, 1976), p. 160.

5. Inrig, p. 48.

6. Ibid., p. 54.

7

Life's Decisions
and the Will of God

*"Any happening, great and small, that is to say,
is a parable whereby God speaks to us; and the
art of life is to get the message."*

—Malcolm Muggeridge

A young man took a job at an orange packing plant because nothing else seemed to be available at the time. All day long he sat at a conveyor belt and sorted oranges into one of three bins according to their size: small, medium or large.

All day long it was the same thing—small, medium or large.

A friend commented, "You absolutely have one of the most boring jobs in the world—nothing to do except sit there and put oranges in a box."

"No," countered the young man. "It is very tiring, but not boring. Decisions, decisions, decisions—it's the decisions that tire me out."

Can you relate to that?

Life is full of decisions.

A generation ago life was a great deal more simple. If you went into a restaurant and ordered a hamburger and a cola, that's exactly what you got. But order the same thing today and you get asked: "What kind of cola do you want? Regular, decaffeinated, diet or cherry?"

"How do you want your hamburger? Rare, medium or well-done (burnt-offering style)?"

"And what kind of a bun would you like? Wheat, white, rye or sourdough?"

You feel like saying, "Look, you're not my mother, and I don't have to answer all those questions. I just want a hamburger and a cola."

I'm sure you will agree that life is not simple. Whether you like it or not, as a single you are forced to make decisions about your future, and when you choose to ignore those decisions, they are made for you. Such "decisions" can be catastrophic.

Question: Where is God in relationship to the decision that you have to make? Does He have a direct will? Or is His will rather nebulous like your father's comment when you were leaving the house, "Now have fun, and don't get into trouble"?

Some singles have grown up with the belief that there is a God and that He has a will for His children, at least in regard to the big decisions of life: perhaps what you do as a career and even possibly the individual that you marry. But, other than that, they feel that God has pretty much left you on your own to make your own decisions and to choose what is best for you as you make your way through the mine fields of relationships in life.

Before you buy into that mind-set, take a look at nature around you; look up at the starry hosts of heaven and learn something of the magnitude of space in relationship to the heavenly bodies; and take a look through a microscope in a laboratory. Notice how the little things of life are so tremendously important and become the structure for the big things.

Even nature itself reveals a pattern of order and precision which reflects the mind of the Creator. Every twenty-four hours the earth rotates on its axis, giving us day and night. The seasons which make life more pleasant are the direct result of the 23.5-degree tilt of the earth on its axis. The atmosphere that surrounds planet earth is in the precise proportion necessary to sustain human life—eighty percent nitrogen and twenty percent oxygen.

If the atmosphere surrounding our planet had more oxygen, you would burn up. If it had less, you would be dead on your feet (worse than you are on Monday morning when the alarm goes off after a busy weekend). A ratio of four parts nitrogen to one part oxygen is just right. Had there been a ratio of two parts nitrogen to one part oxygen, then the atmosphere would be laughing gas (not terribly funny). Two parts nitrogen and two parts oxygen would have produced nitric oxide, and humanity would quickly die from its deadly fumes.

When Jim Irwin, one of the *Apollo 15* astronauts, was chatting with me as we were waiting to do a television program, I said, "Jim, when you were sitting on top of the rocket about to blast into space, did you ever think about the fact that the rocket had been assembled by people who came in with the lowest bid?"

He laughed and said, "I not only thought about it, it scared me half to death!"

One scientist pointed out that if a Saturn rocket had been 99.999 percent foolproof, there would still be 518 working parts subject to failure. Thousands of parts have to fit and work together for the missile to successfully perform. The nightmare of *Apollo 13* showed how great is the danger when just one thing goes wrong. One space mission had to be aborted when a part costing less than $1 malfunctioned.

The Bible says not only that God is interested in your life but that He has a direct will for you and your future. For example, consider these statements: "Do not be foolish, but understand what the Lord's will is" (Ephesians 5:17). In the same book Paul wrote that God "works out everything in conformity with the purpose of his will" (1:11). To the Romans Paul wrote that we are to demonstrate or prove "what God's will is—his good, pleasing and perfect will" (Romans 12:2).

May I anticipate your thinking? *Hey, that stuff may work for other people, but not me.* It may well be that you are missing something important.

Suppose you caught me at the end of a seminar somewhere, and as I was on my way out the door you said, "Harold, I've got a big decision to make. What do you think I should do?" I would listen as carefully as possible, and if I had sufficient information to have an opinion or knew what you should do on the basis of what Scripture tells us, I'd give you my thoughts.

But suppose my son came to me and said, "Dad, I've got to make the biggest decision of my life. Let's talk about it, and then tell me what you think I should do." If I had to stay up all night listening, probing, analyzing and quietly praying for wisdom, I'd do it. What's the difference? It wouldn't be that you are not important. You are.

But Steve is my only son, my flesh and blood. I'd die for him.

Here's the analogy. When you become a believer in Jesus Christ, you become God's child, adopted into the family with the full rights and privileges thereof. You belong to the Father, and the faintest cry of one of His children is important to Him.

As my children were growing up, I let them know very clearly what I expected of them. "You sound like a dictator," you may be saying. No, I sound like a father who loves his children.

"Did they always do what you asked them to do?"

No, of course not. Did you always do what your father asked you to do? They had wills of their own, and that is where the conflict arose.

No matter what the will of the Father is, you have a choice to make: Shall I do what I want to do, or shall I ask the Father to show me clearly what He would have me to do, realizing that He loves me and only wills my best—and then do what He asks?

" 'For I know the plans I have for you,' declares the Lord, 'plans to prosper you and not to harm you, plans to give you hope and a future' " (Jeremiah 29:11).

How Do You Find God's Plan?

A study of the Old Testament indicates that God showed His children His plan in different ways: Sometimes it was by an audible voice, as when Moses was confronted with the burning bush.

Sometimes it was through dreams or visions. Sometimes it was through an angelic messenger, and sometimes it was by casting lots (similar to throwing dice).

It would be nice to hear God's voice audibly saying, "Whatever you do, don't marry that jerk. This time next year, you are going to meet the girl of your dreams, or Mr. Right!"

It would be very helpful to have a dream about the future. Can you trust God for direction through dreams? On the personal side, I'm never quite sure whether it is indigestion or worry that causes some of my dreams to turn to nightmares, especially those in which I find myself doing things that are abhorrent to me, which I would never do as a conscious choice. So don't put a great deal of hope in dreams. Don't expect an angel to stop you from making a fool of yourself, either.

When F.B. Meyer was a passenger on a ship that went from London to Holyhead Harbor in Ireland, he was on the deck when the ship approached the harbor at the end of the journey.

Meyer knew the coast was rocky, and that the harbor itself had varying depths, so when the captain of the ship didn't slow down, he was concerned.

"Captain, how do you know Holyhead Harbor so well?" Meyer asked, which translated means, "Don't you think you should slow down?"

The captain replied, "Do you see those three lights ahead?" pointing out three lights on the hill overlooking the harbor. He explained, "When those three lights all line up in a row, I know that I am in the center of the channel."

Telling of the experience, Meyer used to say, "When we want to know God's will, there are three things which must always concur: the Word of God, the trend of circumstances and the inward impulse of the Holy Spirit."

As a single living in a couples' world, you will find that those three still will give you direction for the future.

1. The direction of God's Word, the Bible

I'm about to write something so radical that you will probably have to stop and think about it before you agree. I say this on the basis of years of study including a Master's and Doctorate degrees in biblical text, as well as on the basis of three decades of experience working with people. Here it is: *The Bible gives direction to us either in principle or in precept (either a direct statement of God's will, or a moral and spiritual framework which provides a principle) for every decision you will have to make in life.*

What about issues like these?

- Should I live with someone who says he loves me very much but is not willing to marry me?
- Because there are so few men, is it OK to marry someone who is not a Christian?
- Should I keep my baby or abort the fetus as my parents want?

- Why not have sex since we intend to marry eventually?
- How much should I tell my mate about my former sexual experiences?
- Should I stay at home and take care of my aged parents?
- Since there aren't many men around here, should I quit my job and go somewhere else?

In the pages of the Bible, you will find many direct (sometimes we wish they were not so direct), specific statements about some of these subjects such as the kind of person you marry, how to treat your parents and show them respect and honor while at the same time you are trying to get on with your life, how to resolve conflicts with others, how to find peace of mind and what to expect in the future.

But you *will not* find specific answers to all of the issues which I just raised. You will, however, find *principles* which give you guidance for each issue. For example, if you check a concordance, you will not find the word abortion listed under "A." You will, however, discover many statements affirming the reality of life in the womb, which then gives you direction regarding the will of God and the reality of the life which you carry within your womb when you are pregnant.

The Bible won't tell you whether to eat that hamburger with all the onions and grease or to opt for a salad with light dressing on it. But it will tell you that your body is the temple of the Holy Spirit and to abuse it by disregarding what is healthful is just as wrong as to abuse it with drugs.

2. The will of God and the witness of the Holy Spirit in your heart

"Earnest Christians seeking guidance often go about it wrong," writes J.I. Packer, a man of God and a person of no small intellect. He says, "Their basic mistake is to think of guidance as essentially an inward prompting of the Holy Spirit, apart from the written Word."[1] The fact is: God does bring a witness within our hearts, one which is never in conflict with the written Word, as to what we should do.

The problem, though, is knowing whether the witness you feel in your heart is *your* will or *God's* will. I'm thinking of a young man who badly needed to make some money, and quickly. He prayed about it and decided that the best way would be to bet on the horse race.

He took the racing card and prayed over it, asking the Lord to please let him pick the winner. He sensed a voice saying, "Seven . . . seven!"

"That's it!" he cried. "The Lord is saying, 'Put your money on the seventh horse in the seventh race!' "

That's exactly what he did! And you know what? The horse came in *seventh!*

To be very honest, do you ever have times when you are uncertain whether the tug you feel in your heart is the result of God's speaking to your heart or is it only the result of your human will? Do you ever have a hard time discerning between the will of God and your own will, or between His voice and the voice of selfish ambition?

There are several questions you can ask yourself that will tell you every time whether the feelings you have in your heart are prompted by the Spirit of God, by your own spirit or even by an unclean, evil spirit.

1. Do I really want God to show me what to do in this matter? This question is really basic. Understand that God doesn't force His will upon you. On the authority of Scripture, I think I can safely say if you really want to know the will of God for your life, you *can* know it.

In his youth while studying in Germany, George Müller was an intellectual who did not believe the Bible. Invited to the home of a friend, Müller heard his host pray after the meal. He was so deeply touched that he went home, got on his knees and was converted. Following his conversion, Müller decided that he would put the promises of the Bible to the test through prayer. Did it work? The simple fact that God answered prayer in ways that were absolutely beyond human explanation not only proved the truth of God's Word to Müller, but also gave him a new direction for his life. He eventually became the founder of orphanages in Britain, and in the course of his lifetime, he never asked for help apart from asking God in prayer to honor the promises of His Word and send in the needed resources.

Writing on the subject of how he found the will

of God for the everyday decisions of life, Müller said:

> I seek at the beginning to get my heart into such a state that it has no will of its own in regard to a given matter. Nine-tenths of the trouble with people is here. Nine-tenths of the difficulties are overcome when our hearts are ready to do the Lord's will, whatever it may be. When one is truly in this state, it is usually but a little way to the knowledge of what His will is.

2. Have I honestly put aside my own will? Can you truthfully say, "Lord, Thy will be done"? In answering that question, it is best to remember that God knows us for what we really are. Our friends and families know us for the image we project, but God knows even the thoughts of our hearts. So often we play games with God. When you can honestly say, "Yes, I know in my heart I am willing to set aside my will in this matter and follow God's direction," you are on your way to the solution.

3. Have I determined that I will accept His direction in my life even though it may be different from what I would choose to do?

It is easier to cheat your way through college than to study hard and pass your exams. It is often easier to be dishonest in order to make a little more money than to tell it like it really is. It is easier to look the other way when somebody needs help than to get involved. When we are serious about our commitment to a loving Heavenly Father, we can fall back on the promise, "I will instruct you and teach you in the way you should go; I will counsel you and watch over you" (Psalm 32:8).

God's will may be different from yours. His will may not always be the easy way out, but with His will comes the enabling power to do what He wants you to do.

Do you remember Paul's pointed words, "Therefore do not be foolish, but understand what the Lord's will is" (Ephesians 5:17)? Making the decision to accept the will of God is a big hurdle, but you can be reasonably sure that God will guide you into His will when you decide you want to do His will in your life.

4. *Is the guidance I feel in my heart in accord with the direction of the Bible?* Be sure of this one thing—there will be times when what you feel in your heart will be contrary to circumstances (which are dictated by logic) but *yet consistent* with what God has already revealed in the Bible. Look at Abraham when God called him to leave the land of Ur and go to a place that God would show him. Can you imagine the consternation that his father, Terah, must have felt when his son said he was leaving?

Could you imagine Terah saying, "Look, Abe, this doesn't make sense. You live in a nice neighborhood. We've got everything you could ask for. What's this business about God leading you away from here? Doesn't make sense to me!" Yet God *was* leading him.

An interesting thing about the Bible is that God has given directions to us which are applicable to every culture and race of people, but quite often that direction is countercultural and certainly contrary to what "everybody else" does.

I am thinking of a tribe I visited in Northern Luzon, Philippines. When young people begin to court each other, if they are serious with each other, they begin having sex. When the girl conceives, the couple then goes to the witch doctor, who says that he thinks their marriage will be fruitful and that they should marry.

That's little different from their counterparts in Europe or America, where couples live together, and after the onset of a pregnancy eventually marry. God's will may be contrary to your culture, and certainly the trends of our day, but it will never be contrary to what He has revealed in His Word, the Bible.

5. Is the guidance, which I feel is prompted by the voice of God's Spirit, confirmed by godly people who are neutral in the whole matter?

When another believer, especially a mature, godly individual, concurs that God is leading you, that concurrence helps to confirm the direction you sense in your heart. Every decision that you make does not have to be confirmed by a "spiritual overseer," but the wisdom of saints, with the experience you may lack, often eliminates uncertainty and gives you confidence to trust God through difficult times. It also helps to prevent some of the stupid things that people have done as they blamed the Holy Spirit for what the flesh dictated.

This conviction of the Holy Spirit, suggests Paul Little,

> is quite different from the 'gung ho' emotion which prods us today to get on a plane to Hong Kong, and tomorrow to move to Chicago. When the Holy Spirit begins to move in our hearts, one conviction deepens and, while we recognize other situations, we sense that this is the will of God for us.[2]

Seeking godly counsel will help you recognize the voice of God's Spirit and avoid self-deception which leads to decisions which you later regret.

The opening and closing of doors is an indication of His will

"Dear God," prayed a young man, "I want patience, and I want it right now." I can relate to that. If I had wanted something tomorrow, I would have waited until then to put in my request. God, however, looks at life through different eyes. He says that His ways and thoughts are different from ours. Does that mean we are on different wavelengths? Yes. Does it mean that He is indifferent to the needs of our lives? Not at all.

The difference is perspective. God sees the end

from the beginning. We see only the immediate. Think of it like this. Visualize an ant crawling on a plank. You reach down and place your hand in front of the ant. All he sees is this impenetrable wall, this huge hand blocking his progress. But you see the entire scene in perspective.

Getting the picture? I am convinced that God, at times, graciously protects us from situations and relationships because He in His wise providence is keeping us from the biggest mistakes of our lives. I'm not suggesting for a moment that you pray, "OK, God, if You don't want me to have that chocolate eclair, then don't let there be a parking place in front of the bakery."

"But I really believed that this was God's will!"

I have no doubt that you do. Some things will never be fully understood this side of heaven, especially when you believe you know what God's will is, but things don't come together. When a few years have separated you from your heartache and your questions, however, you may be able to look back and say, "No matter how much I loved, how much I was hurt when things didn't work out, I now see that God has something different which I could not see at the time."

When God through circumstances closes a door in your life, as painful as it may be, try to look at it as an indication that God *does* have something else—something much better for your life—which you will eventually experience in the future. Until then, you must learn patience, finding that God can give you grace equal to your need.

Does that mean we must say, "Thank You, Lord, for my broken heart!"? Not really. When Paul said we are to "give thanks in all circumstances, for this is God's will . . . in Christ Jesus" (1 Thessalonians 5:18), he was telling us to give thanks that God is great enough, sufficient enough for whatever happens.

Let's consider some of the practical issues which confront you as a single living in a couples' world.

Doing the Right Thing at the Wrong Time

The issue of timing is absolutely critical in life. It isn't how smooth the swing of the baseball player is that counts; it's his timing. Golfers have to learn that the strength of the swing is not as important as how the club makes contact with the ball—timing. In love and marriage, most of our mistakes are the result of not knowing when to do what. Again, timing.

Haste is the parent of nine-tenths of our mistakes. From the days of Abraham, who was in a hurry to help God make the promise of a son a reality, to the couple who says, "Why wait? We're going to get married anyway," issues of timing are critical.

Amsterdam's *De Oude Kerk*, which in Dutch means "The Old Church," dates back to the early sixteenth century. It's the oldest church in the city. Over one of the doors where the marriage commissars of the city assembled, there is an inscription which reads, "Marry in haste, repent in leisure." Perhaps the saying written in Dutch is reflective of the conservative natures of these wise old men, but I think instead it reflected the wisdom of Solomon. If he never said it, he well could have, because Solomon married more than a few women out of political convenience, a practice which he lived to regret.

"Marry in haste, repent in leisure!"—good advice for any generation. No other relationship so involves the totality of your life as does marriage. If people took more time to get to the altar, a great many would never take the trip.

Those who marry in haste are usually guilty of flawed thinking. Consider the following illusions they believe:

Illusion #1: "Things will be better after we are married." To the contrary, traits usually tend to amplify. A man who is kind and considerate becomes more so when you have taken time for a relationship to develop. An individual who is inconsiderate and rude doesn't change into a gentleman or a lady after marriage.

Illusion #2: "It doesn't really matter." Nothing could be more self-deceptive. "Are both of you Christians?" I sometimes ask a couple who want to marry. They look at each other and say, "We've never talked about religion!" When there are major social or cultural differences and those issues have never been addressed, you may have plenty of time to repent in leisure.

When a couple marries, they bring to the altar a large sack containing elements of heredity, habits, culture, idiosyncrasies of temperament and attitude such as "Momma always did it this way." Better take time enough to know what's in the baggage your prospective mate brings to the altar.

Illusion #3: "What you don't know shouldn't bother you." Wrong. The better you know each other and the more able you are to communicate your emotions and feelings, the greater the chance of happiness you have. It's a fact: There is a definite correlation between your contentment in marriage and your ability to communicate at a deep and intimate level. What you don't know about that other person should bother you a great deal. What you find out—too late to do anything about it—may give you a great deal to regret later on.

Illusion #4: "If I don't get him or her now, I may never have another chance to marry." Wrong again. Listen to the testimony of a woman who learned the hard way: "Dear Dr. Sala, Basically I agree with your premise that we should wait for God's choice of a mate. I did not do this and am now going to suffer for the rest of my life."

Illusion #5: Those who marry in haste usually think that love is enough. "We love each other," I hear people say. Thinking of love as a warm emotion which gets the adrenaline flowing, they have never learned that love is a decision, a commitment to care regardless of the temperature of the heart. Real love only grows when the fading beauty writes creases in the forehead and turns the hair gray.

Take time. It may be the most important advice you will ever get.

But What If I Wait Too Long? I Could Miss Out Entirely!

Excuse me, but could I ask, "Miss what?" Miss the heartache of living as two strangers who are never joined together spiritually? Miss going to church by yourself? Miss being treated abusively? Miss the pain of wishing your husband or wife would be intimate and open with you? Thanks, but no thanks.

If there is one thing that is far worse than being single (if you consider being single in that light), it to be married to the wrong person. Take, for example, these words: "Dear Dr. Sala, You imply that God will provide a mate. You cannot assume this. I have a woman friend who did what you suggested—trusted God to send her a husband and she turned down eligible men. Now she is sixty, unmarried and bitter toward God."

There are situations where eligible Christian men are very scarce. Thousands of Filipinas have come to the United States where they can make salaries many times that of their professional counterparts in the Philippines. Naturally preferring to marry someone whose culture is compatible with their own, they would like to marry Filipinos who have the same value system and outlook on life.

The men don't exist in equal numbers because of immigration policies.

Of course, the women are frustrated. "What can we do?" they ask.

There are three options:

Option #1: Go home where you will come into contact with a far greater number of men who fit the requirements for a serious relationship.

Option #2: Change employment, preferably moving to another city (where the situation may not be any different from where you are).

Option #3: Realize that you are working and living where you are because this is God's plan for you, at least for today. You can trust Him to meet your needs.

Does God Have a Plan for My Life and a Man for My Plan?

I would never go beyond what Scripture says, and there is not even a suggestion that God has a "man for every plan." What He has promised, however, is to meet your needs. "And my God will meet all your needs according to his glorious riches in Christ Jesus," says Paul whose words are recorded in Philippians 4:19.

Whether you need a husband or a wife is an issue between you and God. I can, however, tell you of those who did have that need and how God met them.

Dave Morrow believes you can trust God for His provision when you are doing what He wants you to do. Dave was raised on the mission field in Africa, and after he completed his seminary training he took a position in a local church, still searching for the right one who could go back to Africa with him.

He kept looking over the crowd every Sunday morning to see if a new face had appeared. Finally he asked my advice, "What do you think I should do?"

"What do you think God wants you to do with your life?" I inquired.

"I think God wants me in Africa," he responded.

I said, "Then you had better get moving that direction."

Sudan Interior Mission, the group that Dave was serving, needed him on a rather remote outstation a distance from Addis Ababa. "Great chance of finding a wife there!" people told Dave. Nonetheless, he went.

Meanwhile an Australian nurse felt called by God into medical missions. She was single but hoped to meet someone who shared her vision of missionary medicine. Nobody even came close to being the answer. Finally she joined the same mission Dave had joined. They told her about a medical work in a pretty remote area outside Addis Ababa. Her family and friends told her, "If you go there, you'll end up being an old maid for sure."

Putting the will of God above "finding the right man," she packed and went to Africa. You guessed it. They met, fell in love and married. Both of them could so easily have missed God's best for their lives had they gotten ahead of God.

John and Shannon Haslett would agree. After several years of short-term missions, both, as singles, agreed to go to Africa with Youth With A

Mission. "Where are you from?" John asked Shannon when they met. She replied, mentioning the same town where he lived.

"Really?" he replied, surprised. "What's your address there?"

She told him. Amazed, he replied, "That's exactly where I have been living!"

Believe it or not, they both had lived in the same apartment complex in the same city, on the same street, but had to go 7,000 miles away to meet each other, fall in love, marry and have a family.

But What If I Missed God's Plan Back When . . . ?

Recently I was on my way to speak to a church on Sunday morning, happily driving down the freeway, my coffee mug nestled by the gear shift, listening to beautiful music, thinking about God's goodness and having a great time.

Suddenly I felt something warm on my pant leg. The entire mug of coffee had turned over, soaking the floor mat and by means of osmosis was creeping up my pant leg.

I was under attack. I kept driving as I grabbed a rag and attempted to sop up the coffee. The next thing I knew I looked up and noticed that I had gone at least five miles beyond the place where I was to turn.

I had blown it. So what did I do? Slam on the brakes, throw the car in reverse and back up for five miles? Not on your life.

I paused and asked, "How do I get there from here?"

That's the question you have to ask yourself when you realize that somewhere—in a night of passion when reason took a vacation, when your brain went out your ear for a drink of water and didn't come back, when you wanted to believe what your hormones were telling you—you missed God's plan.

Now you must say, "OK, God, I blew it. I confess that. I want Your forgiveness, and I want You to show me how to get where You want me to go with my life."

But What If I Still Don't Know What to Do?

If that is the case, there is only one issue to consider. Ask, "What does God want me to do *today?*" Then get to work doing it. When I was a young man in my early twenties, and I was searching for God's plan for my life, Paul Finkenbinder told me, "God's will is like a flashlight in a dungeon; it doesn't shine around corners. It doesn't illuminate the next cave; it only gives you enough light for the next step."

The important thing is not necessarily, "What does God want me to do five years from now?" but rather, "What does He want me to do five minutes from now?"

Don't avoid your responsibilities today, while pondering the great questions about tomorrow. If you know the next step—even though it may be a very short one—take it.

Rest assured that God is seldom early, but He is never late. Corrie ten Boom used to recall that when she was a little girl and had to get on the train, her father never gave her the ticket until it was time to board. Trust God for the ticket to happiness and accomplishment today and leave tomorrow to Him. Remember the words of Ecclesiastes 3:11, "He has made everything beautiful in its time. He has also set eternity in the hearts of men; yet they cannot fathom what God has done from beginning to end."

Endnotes

1. J.I. Packer, *The 1987 Great Commission Handbook*, p. 72.

2. Paul Little, "Affirming the Will of God," *The 1992 Great Commission Handbook*, p. 25.

8

If You Should Leave the Ranks of Singles

"Keep your eyes open before marriage;
half-shut afterward."

—Benjamin Franklin

*K*eeping your eyes wide open before you marry is good advice based on the growing number of marriage fatalities today. The fact is that most people only *think* they know the person they meet at the altar, and then after the honeymoon is over, they wake up one day and say, "This is not the person that I thought I was marrying. I am living with a stranger, and I want out!"

An acquaintance of mine was flying on a plane and noticed that the man sitting in the seat next to him wore his wedding ring on his middle finger—a rather strange thing since most men wear wedding rings on their fourth finger (an age-old custom stemming from the belief that a vein ran from this finger straight to the heart).

"You know, it's none of my business," he commented, "but I notice you have your wedding ring on the wrong finger."

"Yep, I married the wrong girl!"

Before you say, "Yes!" to marriage, ask yourself ten questions which can well help you determine if your relationship has what it takes to bring happiness and fulfillment and give you a good marriage. If you are presently in a relationship which may culminate in marriage, working through these issues is an absolute must.

Question #1: Do we share a common faith in Jesus Christ?

Amazingly, as they approach marriage many couples never discuss their views on God, what church they will attend and what part Christ will play in their lives. Your concept of God and your commitment to what the Bible says affect every part of your life: how you raise your children, how you conduct business, even how you celebrate your love together.

"There's something I must tell you before we are married," said one young man as their wedding day approached.

"Yes, dear," said the young woman.

"I'm an insomniac [someone who can't sleep]."

Pensively thinking about this new revelation, she replied, "All right, you go to your church and I'll go to mine!"

When you are influenced by the passion of love, you seldom want to consider the way your faith affects your adjustment to life together, either negatively or positively.

God knew that two people whose level of spiritual commitment is the same can have a far deeper personal relationship. It was for this reason that Paul wrote, "Do not be yoked together with unbelievers. For what do righteousness and wickedness have in common? Or what fellowship can light have with darkness?" (2 Corinthians 6:14).

Paul's advice is the application of an injunction in the law that forbade putting an ox and a donkey side by side harnessed to a plow (see Deuteronomy 22:10). The two have different strengths and temperaments. Likewise when two marry and have not only different spiritual views but even different levels of spiritual commitment, they are unequally yoked and will face significant problems. It's not that one goes to church and the other sleeps in on Sundays. It's not even that one wants to say grace at the table, and the other says, "Do we have to pray at every meal like a bunch of religious fanatics?" It's how they view life. The whole perspective is different.

Question #2: What do we have in common?

Does the answer include music, art, sports, literature, television, activities, involvement in church or Christian service? Once the honeymoon is over, it is the common interests which you share which become the glue that keeps your relationship healthy and vibrant. Romance doesn't have to take second place, but good marriages need glue stronger than sex to make them work. It's your common interests which keep you moving together. Two individuals who are attracted to each other because both are from unhappy homes or backgrounds seldom find happiness by marrying another unhappy person. Eventually misery begins to feed off the other person and it multiplies.

There's another issue you need to think about. Opposites attract but too much opposition repels.

- He loves country western music; she loves classical.
- He is a sports addict; she thinks that grown men pushing each other around is ridiculous.
- He loves the outdoors; she enjoys concerts outdoors and not much more.
- He wants to sleep with the windows open; she wants them closed.
- He thinks it is OK to burp out loud; she is mortified when that happens.
- He is a "free spirit" type who never plans ahead; she has her organizer and works it religiously.

At times you are attracted to a person because that individual is strong in the very areas where you are weak. *We'd make a great team,* you think. Yet the reality is that living with someone who is substantially different from you isn't always easy. There has to be an area of common interests at the core of your relationship large enough to help you cope with the differences.

Question #3: Can I love this person as he or she is now?

Putting the question another way, ask yourself if you must remake this person into the individual you want him or her to be. Can you be happy waking up in the morning for the rest of your life knowing that the first person you will see is this one you have been thinking about marrying?

Counseling couples who are thinking of marriage, I remind them that there are three words that are in the mind of the bride: aisle (the long one she will walk down dressed in white), altar (where they will take their vows) and hymn (the song which will be sung at the wedding). But after the wedding those words get spelled, "I'll," "alter" and "him": "I'll change him."

Thinking that marriage will change an individual who is thoughtless or careless into a thoughtful, caring individual who is committed to you is foolish thinking. A rule of thumb is this: "As now, so then, but more so." In other words, a person who is thoughtful and caring before marriage will be even more so after you are married. If someone tends to be abusive and puts you down before you are married, that individual will do more of it afterward. Marriage only intensifies the qualities a person has.

If the love of a person for you before marriage is not sufficiently strong to produce the changes— genuine changes which you feel are important— during your courtship, don't expect change to come after you are married. I stress that change must be genuine because it is easy for some—especially a man—to appear to have become what you hope he is, when, in fact, his behavior is a charade which will quickly revert back after marriage to what he was before.

On the other hand, sociologists working with

delinquents have found that the love of a girl is one of the most powerful motivational factors which produce lasting change in men. It's the power of real love.

Question #4: What attracts me to this person?

Is the attraction an inner beauty? Is it that he is handsome or rich? Or she has a great figure and a pretty smile? Or am I really drawn to this person because I see a radiance within which goes far beyond looks and I find that I am a better person when I am with her or him?

An old adage goes, "Beauty is skin deep," and a chauvinist male added, "Yep, but ugly goes clear to the bone." Both are true in a different sense. Physical beauty may not necessarily be an asset—unless you consider attention by members of the opposite sex to be an asset. One of the most beautiful girls I ever knew sadly took her life at the age of twenty-five after three unsuccessful marriages. "Men think of me strictly as a sex object," she said.

Before scientists had invented the smallpox vaccine, Blaise Pascal said, "If a man loves a woman for her beauty, does he love her? No. For the smallpox, which destroys her beauty without killing her, causes his love to cease."[1]

From the present perspective of nearly four decades of marriage, I can honestly say that when you really love someone, with the passing of years a person grows even more beautiful year after year.

"Will you love your wife when she gets old and gray?" a friend asked.

"I should. I've loved her through five colors already."

That's the kind of attraction which keeps a husband coming home night after night.

Question #5: Does this person complement me and add to my life, or is our relationship a one-way transaction?

The time to ask this very important question is when your relationship begins to move from the friendship stage to the more intimate level of understanding.

A certain golfer got home several hours late and someone asked why the game took so long.

He explained, "Well, you know George, my best friend? He had a heart attack and died on the seventh hole, and after that it was hit the ball and drag George, hit the ball and drag George."

Sometimes I see relationships which are just like that. One of the two hits the ball down the fairway of life and constantly pulls the other. While I may admire the emotional strength of one who helps carry the relationship, I also sense the tremendous emotional drain which takes place in the life of the stronger person. I also can't help thinking how much happier that one would have been had he or she married someone else—or stayed single.

For those who have already married someone such as I've described, it is too late. But for you who are considering marriage, take inventory. Does the other person enhance your personality? Does he or she bring out the best in you? Or does he or she drain your emotional strength and productive energies?

Mary met Joe when they were both working at the same restaurant. Both, they discovered, went to the same church, though they didn't know each other in that setting. Mary knew that Joe's health was not very good, but they were good friends. Then the relationship deepened, and Joe proposed. At that point he had to tell her that he was HIV positive and that this would affect their life together.

OK, he wasn't fair with her in not being up-front and telling her this before she fell in love with him, but that doesn't change her feelings. Does she say, "Hey, you deceived me. I can't handle this!" or does she say, "I love you and I'll live with the consequences"?

At that point Mary needs counseling and serious thinking because she will be the one who ends up being a primary caregiver in that relationship. Her own health as well as her future is involved.

Whether it is health, habits, personal idiosyncrasies or just attitudes, ask whether the other complements you or whether you have to constantly help pull the other out of depression or trouble.

Question #6: Do we share common views on commitment?

Are we both committed to the words which we vow when we say, "I take you . . . till death us do part"? Or do we interpret this as, "I take you . . . as long as we both shall agree" which usually doesn't last through the honeymoon? When I do family seminars, I often ask, "What in your opinion is the most important single ingredient that goes into a relationship?"

Most people say, "Love!"

And I have to tell them that love is number three on my list, behind commitment and communication. Here's why. Without a deep and abiding commitment to a marriage, people don't care enough to communicate at a deep and intimate level, and without communication love begins to wither and die.

The kind of commitment which is necessary is the kind that you *live,* which says, in effect, "God brought us together, and come hell or high water, no matter what problems we may face, some way, somehow, we're going to trust God for a solution."

In that kind of a relationship, a broken home is never an option. Divorce is not a problem-solving technique. On the contrary, when your personality is flawed or when you are immature and selfish, changing partners isn't the answer. It is you who must change.

It is when commitment begins to weaken that

you stop working on a relationship and begin to consider options which God never intended.

Question #7: Are our family backgrounds compatible?

"I'm not marrying her *family*; I'm marrying *her!*" Actually, you are marrying both. When a couple stands at a marriage altar, they both bring along large gunny sacks. Inside are habits, the force of heredity, idiosyncrasies of personality and temperament, and sometimes a lot of emotional garbage from the past—all of which affect how you relate to each other.

In recent years I have also come to see that problems which arise in cross-cultural marriages are similar to the unequal yoking described in Question #1, even in relationships where both are believers. I first was confronted with this in Liberia, a nation which was established during the tenure of the American President James Madison, who sent slaves from America back to Africa to establish a colony.

When Liberian men came to the United States to study, met African-American women and then took them back to their home in Liberia, the rate of marriage failure was over the ninety percent mark. Both had common roots, both spoke the same language. Why such a dismal rate of marriage failure?

People explained, "It's the culture!" Liberian families rejected the brides with, "You don't understand us. You didn't grow up here." The American women had severe difficulty integrating into the culture.

Lest I be misunderstood, I am not suggesting that cross-cultural marriages fall in the same category as marriage to an unbeliever. But I am saying cross-cultural relationships are challenged by differences in habits, attitudes, practices and mannerisms. Should you be considering marrying someone from a different culture, take time to work through all of these issues.

When an American marries a Filipino, I explain to the American that he or she is not marrying a person, but a family. The ceremony should read, "I take you, your mother and father, your siblings and friends, to be my wedded wife (or husband)!" The responsibilities to the family are much deeper and more intensive in Filipino families than in American families.

Not understanding that, the American male marries and a home is established in the United States. Then when her family comes for an extended visit he begins to chafe, wishing they would move out or go home. His wife, though, is perfectly happy. She knows that this reciprocal responsibility is part of her commitment to her parents and family. That's when the fur begins to fly.

The situation involving cross-cultural marriages, though, goes far beyond the how-long-your-family-stays-as-house-guests issue to how you relate to each other, what men do or, as the case usually is, *don't do* and vice versa.

When Darlene and I drove through the lovely Austrian countryside, we came to the spot where the Rhine and the Enn Rivers flow together—two massive rivers carrying lots of water. As we stood at the confluence of these two great rivers we noticed that for almost as far as we could see there was turbulence as the waters mingled. Further downstream they flowed peacefully, but this took time. So is it with relationships.

Though you often don't think about it, when two lives come together you are blending both heredity and environment—both nature and nurture. The Bible says that "you become one flesh," not "you are one flesh."

This "becoming" takes time and involves the commitment to give and take (*not* you give and I take).

Ask yourself if your two families seem to share the same values, the same economic structure, the same habits and goals.

One of the saddest funerals I ever conducted was that of a young woman in her late twenties who took her own life. Having never met her husband before, I assumed that she had been depressed and sick. "How long has your wife been ill?" I asked.

"She wasn't sick," he said, adding, "She knew exactly what she was doing."

He explained that his family was quite wealthy, and she was from a very ordinary background. His family would not accept her—she was beneath their social standing. "It was more than she could handle," he sadly related.

At the funeral when the mourners filed past the open casket, his family would not even look at the face of the young lady who lay there—a victim of their snobbery and indifference.

It's a good thing that I'm not God because they wouldn't have walked out of there alive if I had been filling in for Him that morning.

Again, this is not to say that your Prince Charming cannot have been born with a silver spoon in his mouth, but if he was, you better be sure that you can meet the expectations of his family and that they accept you for who you are.

Question #8: Am I willing to be treated as his or her parents treat each other?

Is this important? You bet it is. We tend to replay in our marriages what we have grown up with, what we have seen firsthand at home. The person who grows up in a broken home is more likely to have a broken home of his own—in spite of knowing the heartache and anguish of living in a home without love between a father and a mother.

Are you willing to be treated as his dad treats his mother? That's how he probably will treat you after you are married. His dad was his role model. And likewise, she learned from her mother.

When Carlos was growing up, he saw constant, open conflict between his parents. When there was disagreement, his dad would walk out, sometimes being gone for a week. They never learned how to resolve issues other than explode, back off and then "kiss" without really making up.

He married a girl much like his mother who also had a will of her own. After the first couple of years, they began to have serious disagreements. The issue primarily was that of control. Both Carlos and Nancy were afraid of "losing the argument." Subsequently, Carlos, when he began to realize Nancy was better with words than he, would revert back to what he had seen his dad do—walk out!

For this couple, Marriage Encounter (a seminar in which couples explore marital issues together) helped them learn to express feelings instead of making accusations. It helped save their marriage.

Question #9: How does this person respond to trouble and pressure?

Unlike the courtship which is often grossly unrealistic—everything is more glamorous than real life—marriage and life are reality. We live in an imperfect, broken world. Things happen.

- People get laid off.
- Doctors say, "You have cancer, and we must remove your breast."
- Men are hit by lightning on the golf course or get struck by a car as they are changing a flat tire on the freeway.
- Automobile accidents leave your face scarred.
- Your health collapses.

- Babies tumble into swimming pools and drown.
- Illness strikes.
- Immigration cancels your visa.

How does the one you are thinking about marrying respond to pressure and stress? Can it be faced? When there is a disagreement, can he or she say, "I really am sorry. Please forgive me. I accept responsibility for what happened"? Or is the person a "no-faulter"—the kind that always has to place the blame on someone else (probably you) for what happened?

When difficulty strikes, does it drive you into each other's arms, and then you both turn to the Lord? When a tragedy strikes—say the accidental death of a child—it puts a tremendous strain on a relationship, and in many cases, that strain is more than a marriage can handle.

When Ruth was diagnosed with cancer and a mastectomy was scheduled, Bill walked out on her. "I just can't handle it," he said. But Ruth said, "If ever I needed his support, it was then—the lowest point of my life."

Because we live in an imperfect world, we have to learn how to cope with stress, how to reach out to the Lord in prayer and draw inner strength from our Heavenly Father instead of playing the blame game or turning and running. Nobody ever outruns trouble, so you had better learn to cope with it.

Question #10: Do I really know this person?

"But we have been together practically day and night for two years!"

So what?

When I ask if you really know the person involved, I am not asking if you know the color of her eyes (you'd be blind if you didn't) or the flavor of her lipstick or even the size of his shoe.

Do you let each other see beneath the veneer to know what is inside? Bottom line: Do you communicate with each other at a deep and intimate level? Can he share feelings with you? Are you secure enough in his love that you can share your fears with him and not worry that you will be rejected?

"Dear, you never tell me how you feel!"

"Yes, I do. Just yesterday I told you that I *felt* like I was catching a cold."

When it comes to troubled marriages, almost all of them share a common problem: the lack of effective communication. Men and women communicate, using the same words, in what amounts to an entirely different language. Men generally communicate from a logical or rational vantage point, women from an emotional one; yet for both, communication skills can be developed when the desire to learn is stronger than the complacency which keeps you from learning it.

But You Haven't Talked about Love. Isn't That Important?

Yes, very important, and that's why I have saved this topic for a final discussion before the last chapter of the book.

When Darlene and I lived in the Philippines in the early '70s, we worked with a number of couples whose marriages had basically been arranged by parents, usually with the thought of controlling the family fortune. As much as my cultural background opposed the concept, I gradually began to realize that this was not an entirely bad idea.

Parents who knew the relative strengths and weaknesses of their children could quite accurately predict the success or failure of a given relationship. I discovered that two individuals whose marriage was not necessarily founded on the basis of romantic love and attraction could and did learn to really love each other. Now, almost a generation later, the individuals that I have kept in contact with have good homes. They are active in their churches. They obviously did learn to love each other.

But I can tell you one thing for sure: They will not be able to arrange the marriages of their children. That idea today is about as popular as a ham sandwich in a Jewish synagogue. It just won't fly. Today the stress is on personal choice and individual preference.

Of those who have responded to a *Guidelines* survey on singles and how they think, ninety-three percent said they would not marry someone they did not love. What surprised me was the seven percent who said they *would* marry someone whom they did not love.

What is love? Earlier in this book I said that love is an unconditional commitment to an imperfect individual to meet the needs of that person in a way that requires personal sacrifice.

Love is a decision, a commitment to care—not simply an emotional state of mind caused by raging hormones. Think about the following ten assumptions and rate them as true or false.

1. The most important thing, when it comes to love and happiness, is picking the right partner. Answer: False. Picking the right partner is only one factor. Being the right partner is even more essential. Most problems in marriage are not with the other person but with yourself. Most people want the other person to change but are unwilling to bend themselves.

2. Few people agree on what love really is. Answer: False. A study of more than 1,000 young men and women demonstrates that love means the same thing to most of us.

3. Being intelligent is a handicap to love. Answer: False. Studies indicate that individuals with intelligence have a greater capacity to change and adapt to the circumstances of a relationship. In simple terms, they are secure enough that winning every argument is not that important.

4. Absence makes a heart grow fonder. Answer: False. The reality is that absence causes the heart to wander. Being together is vital to resolving differences and to growing more intimate with each other. Separation makes communication more difficult and a relationship more strained. Absence tends to foster romantic notions, but in reality it doesn't help a relationship to grow.

5. *People who believe in romantic love are more apt to be emotionally unstable.* Answer: False. Studies at a major university show that individuals with little sense of romance tend to be "rigid, inhibited individuals." But people who can enjoy a walk in the moonlight or are willing to spend some money on perfume or flowers are better adjusted and more willing to contribute to a relationship.

6. *Men are more willing to let their heads rule their hearts than women are.* Answer: False. The fact is that having said "I do!" women are far more interested in material considerations such as a nice home and furniture, a good car and social status. (Of course, men are not falling over themselves to talk about what's going on in their hearts.)

7. *The strong, silent male is more likely to be a great lover than the outgoing verbal one.* Answer: False. The American Institute of Family Relations studies show that the fortunes of love "strongly influence the man who is most fluent in expressing his feelings. A 'strong, silent' disposition was found to be a definite handicap." The bottom line: The strong silent male is apt to have real trouble in expressing his love.

8. There are two periods of life—teen years and in your early forties—when you are most apt to fall in love. Answer: True. For men, however, this occurs a bit later (late teens and early twenties and their mid-forties).

9. If you really love someone, success is pretty certain in marriage. Answer: False. Much more than love is necessary to make a marriage work. Love is only one of the ingredients.

10. To be happy in a loving relationship, you need to put your best foot forward. Answer: False. Being completely honest and vulnerable is vitally necessary if you are to know and really love the other person.

A Closing Thought

There are no guarantees when it comes to your future happiness, but you can be reasonably sure that if you come up with "good" answers to these ten tough questions, you will find the contentment you really want.

In this final chapter, however, I don't want to focus on "future happiness" somewhere out there provided certain things happen. I want to focus on your contentment and fulfillment now, this moment. Keep reading.

Endnote

1. Blaise Pascal as quoted by Ray Mossholder, *Singles Plus* (Lake Mary, FL: Creation House, 1994), p. 131.

9

Don't Worry—
Be Happy!

"Unable to conceive of a God who does not regard human happiness as the be-all and end-all of creation, the practitioners of 'I'm OK, You're OK' spirituality cannot accept the central paradox of religious faith: that the secret of happiness lies in renouncing the right to be happy."

—Christopher Lasch

"*D*on't worry—be happy!" says the host of a popular radio talk show. And why not? Doesn't everybody want to be happy? As Robert Louis Stevenson wrote, "The world is so full of a number of things, I'm sure we should all be as happy as kings."

But the fact is, we are not always happy. Some way, we've been convinced that

1. Happiness is an attainable goal, and
2. When you have certain things—usually associated with power, wealth or achievement—then you will be happy.

How would you finish this statement: "If I just had _____, I would be happy!"

__ If I just got married, I'd be happy . . .
__ If I could just get these creditors off my back . . .
__ If my health improved . . .
__ If I just had a better figure . . .
__ If I could just get _____ to look at me . . .
__ If I had that promotion . . .

We make everything depend on the conditional "if ": "If this would happen" or "If I could have (whatever), I'd be happy."

Are We Entitled to "Happy"?

Happiness in life is conditional. It is usually dependent on your circumstances, your environment, your achievements and your pleasure. Like a beautiful sunset that gradually fades into dusk, happiness is usually momentary and fleeting. Has our culture placed far too much emphasis on happiness as a "right" which we deserve? Have we bought into the mentality that God owes us a chunk of happiness, and if we aren't happy, then it's His fault?

One cold February a *Guidelines* listener wrote, "Doctor, how can we be happy here in Wisconsin when the mercury drops down to fifty-two below as it did the middle of January and the wind chill factor was minus seventy-two?"

If those attain happiness who live in the tropics and never have to shovel snow, I might concede his point. In the tropics people gripe because "nothing stays cold" and the cockroaches proliferate at an incredible rate. In cold countries people complain because it's never warm. Is there no middle ground where everyone is happy all the time?

I am thinking of a speaker I heard recently. He began by asking, "Are you a happy person? On a scale of one to ten, how happy are you?" He continued with seven steps to happiness, occasionally weaving in a Scripture verse. The speaker was on the staff of a prominent seminary, and he is recognized as a Christian psychologist who is supposed to have a handle on both God and the best of psychology. What he said left me with the popular notion that God wants His children happy all of the time, and that if you are not happy, you are missing something important, something to which you are entitled, something which God wants for you. I came away feeling that either something was grossly wrong with me or else our friend wasn't quite on dead center.

Most people feel that "life, liberty and the pursuit of happiness" are rights which everyone should have, guaranteed by both God and government. But are they really? I've been thinking a good deal about happiness in relationship to God. Should happiness be the goal of every single living in a couples' world?

I've been asking myself how happy some of God's choicest servants were whose lives are chronicled by both Scripture and history.

Take Paul, for instance. Suppose a reporter for the local newspaper cornered him at the Jerusalem Straw Hat Pizza parlor any time after his conversion and asked, "Brother Paul, we're doing some interviews with people who make the news, and you're name is quite often in the *Christian Gazette.* We'd like to ask you on a scale of one to ten, how happy are you?"

I think Paul might look somewhat amazed. "You've got to be kidding, friend. Happy? Are you serious? Let me read you a paragraph of this letter which I just wrote to some friends in Corinth. Remember, that's where I got arrested and brought to court. Here it is: 'We are hard pressed on every side, but not crushed; perplexed, but not in despair; persecuted, but not abandoned; struck down, but not destroyed. We always carry around in our body the death of Jesus, so that the life of Jesus may also be revealed in our body' (2 Corinthians 4:8-10)."

Paul might add, "If happiness were my goal, I'd forget Christianity, buy a villa on the Mediterranean and write motivational books. I could make big money doing that. Now, if you were asking about joy or peace amidst the storms of life, that would be quite another matter."

Have you ever thought much about Jesus and happiness? Reading His biography in the New Testament, do you get the feeling that happiness didn't figure largely in the scheme of what He considered to be important? Do you think He ever was tempted to suggest to the multitudes that if they were unhappy, they hadn't received everything that God had for them? Some way, I cannot conceive of Jesus prefacing one of His messages with the question, "On a scale of one to ten, how happy are you?"

At the same time, read something of church history and ask yourself if happiness was the goal of men and women who walked with God. Did happiness figure largely in the lives of the disciples or St. Augustine or the reformers who faced the hostility of established religion and government?

The Happiness/Joy Confusion

Are we being misled today by those who suggest

that happiness is part of the birthright of all God's children, and if you are not happy, is God indeed withholding something important, something to which you are rightfully entitled?

If the answer to that question is, "Yes," does this mean that God wants you *unhappy?* That He wants you to wear black and drink vinegar? Not at all! We're confused today because we think that joy and happiness are synonymous; and using the values system of a godless world, we've put a premium on happiness which is not biblical.

One of the last articles which came from the pen of Oxford professor C.S. Lewis was entitled, "We have No Right to Happiness." Said Lewis, "A right to happiness doesn't make much more sense than a right to be six feet tall, or to have a millionaire for a father, or to get good weather whenever you want to have a picnic."[1] Though the article basically attacked the impulse to walk out on an unhappy marriage because of what people consider to be their "right to happiness," Lewis went beyond that. He said that though "our technological skill may help us to survive a little longer, our civilization will have died at heart and will be swept away" when happiness becomes our driving quest and goal in life.

There is something far more important than happiness—it is joy—and happiness is the world's substitute. Like the Easter Bunny, which is the world's substitute for the resurrection, and Santa Claus, who replaces the baby Jesus in the manger, the world's idea of happiness is a poor substitute, a parody of that joy which you as a Christian can have through a God-dimension, a spiritual relationship which the unregenerated cannot have.

What's the difference? Try these for size.

- Happiness is dependent on circumstances; joy transcends them. (You can be joyful when you aren't happy.)
- Happiness involves your environment—your home, your money, your friends, your health—but joy is internal; it comes from within.
- Happiness is usually temporary (nothing stays forever) but joy abides and remains when beauty fades.
- Happiness has very little to do with God; joy has everything to do with Him.
- Happiness is material; joy is spiritual.
- Happiness involves your life here and now; joy includes both time and eternity.

Affirmation #1: I will accept myself as a person of value and worth.

That's God's point of view, and understanding who you really are frees you to be everything that God intends you to be. It's first and fundamental. Accepting this truth puts distance between you and some of the issues which create unhappiness in the lives of singles.

Affirmation #2: I will submit my will to the will of God regarding marriage.

This is an issue of control—who is in charge of your life? When you believe that God can be trusted, you can also say, "Lord, You know the needs of my life far better than I, so instead of worrying about the future and the issue of marriage, I will rest in the confidence that You will give me guidance, wisdom and a sense of peace as I strive to live just one day at a time."

Affirmation #3: I would rather be in the will of God and single than out of the will of God and married.

For some the will of God means singleness; for others marriage. When you make doing the will of God your goal, God will bring into your life the people whom He would have you to meet. That's the way relationships can develop.

Affirmation #4: I refuse to feel sorry for myself or feel that I am less than a whole person.

As a single you can do many things that married people usually cannot, especially when children come into the picture—sleep till noon, play tennis, travel, spend time with friends, do missionary service. That's Paul's point in First Corinthians 7. A married person spends time pleasing a mate but a single can spend more time pleasing the Lord. The single life is far less cluttered than married life. The point is that you don't need anything to be complete. You are there right now.

Affirmation #5: I will celebrate my singleness in Christ.

If you are not very good company for yourself, the first thing I would suggest is that you sit down and take a good look at yourself. Write down your good qualities, things that you do well. Take a good look at areas at which you excel. Discover your uniqueness, then notice what it allows you to do which you could never accomplish as a married person. It's OK to enjoy yourself.

Affirmation #6: I will sublimate my sexual energies into productive channels.

Sublimating sexual energies means a de-emphasis on sexually orientated materials—movies, what you read, what you watch, what you think about. It's what Paul was driving at when he talked about keeping his body under control and bringing it into subjection (see 1 Corinthians 9:27). Next to keeping the dragon of loneliness at bay, this will probably be your greatest struggle. Every day, make the conscious decision to let thoughts of sex be subject to your will.

Affirmation #7: I will refuse to allow bitterness to creep into my life.

Paul's second letter to the Corinthians is one of the warmest and most intimate of all the letters which came from this remarkable man. Scholars call it "the heart of Paul," because in this autobiographical work he shares his joys and his frustrations. Though singleness does not make the list, he admits to being vulnerable and very human. "We are hard pressed on every side," he writes, and the word which Paul used speaks of pressure. We are "perplexed, but not in despair" he adds, using a term that indicates he was just plain confused about some things. "I thought someone like Paul would have it all figured out!" No, there are some things in life which we won't fully understand until we get to heaven.

We are "persecuted, but not abandoned," he says, and "struck down, but not destroyed," using a word which was also used of the soil which was packed down when the foundation of a building was to be laid (see 2 Corinthians 4:8-9). Yet Paul could say, "Therefore we do not lose heart" (4:16).

How could he cope without growing bitter?

1. He practiced daily renewal: "Though outwardly we are wasting away, yet inwardly we are being renewed day by day" (4:16).
2. He kept his perspective: "We fix our eyes not on what is seen, but on what is unseen. For what is seen is temporary, but what is unseen is eternal" (4:18).

The circumstances you do not like will eventually accomplish one of two things: prove to be a blessing in disguise or eventually produce bitterness. Bitterness or blessing is a choice which you make either as an act of your will or by default.

Affirmation #8: I will make Jesus Christ Lord of all my life.

What does this mean? Join a church? Wear a crucifix? Go into a convent or a monastery? Or does it mean something totally different, something which affects the way I live, the way I think, the way I approach life?

When the disciples called Jesus "Lord," it was obvious that they were using more than just a polite term of respect such as we would use by calling someone Mister or Sir. They believed that He was God, uniquely different from them yet facing the same temptations and difficulties.

This was the issue which finally brought Him into confrontation with the religious leaders of His day. He claimed to be God, saying, "Before Abraham was born, I am!" (John 8:58)—the implication being "I am God."

When you acknowledge Christ as Lord, you not only are embracing Him as Savior and God, you are also coming to grips with the issue of who is in control of your life. You are submitting to His authority and allowing Him to direct your life.

Fear is the cause of much of our concern in this regard. "Can I submit to Him and be confident that He will bring good things into my life?" Your concern reminds me of the young man who came to Diogenes, a Greek philosopher, and said, "I want to become your follower."

"Good," said Diogenes. "Here are two fish; carry them in your tunic and come back in three weeks."

In three days, cats were following the young man down the street.

In a week his parents had asked him to leave home. They couldn't stand the smell.

In ten days he came back, threw the smelly, rotten fish at the feet of Diogenes and said, "I cannot stand it another day. I quit!"

"What tremendous dedication," says the philosopher, "and all lost over two smelly fish."

The moral: God is a good God who doesn't take delight in our misery or discomfort. He never insists that we carry dead, smelly fish in our pockets to prove our devotion or loyalty to Him.

Do you remember the issue Paul Little raised which I discussed in chapter 2, "Is God a good God?" When you settle that issue, it becomes easier to say, "Jesus, I bow my knee to You and ask You to be Lord of my life."

Here's a practical application of what this means.

One day in the near future, there will be a new head of state in Great Britain. Probably Queen Elizabeth will step down and her son Prince Charles will become king. When that happens there will be an assembly in Westminster Abbey of royalty from all over the world and the heads of state from other nations.

Before the crown is placed on the head of the queen's successor, in a ceremony that is centuries old, the Archbishop of Canterbury will turn to the assembly and say, "Sires, I present to you Prince Charles, your rightful king. Are you ready to pay homage?"

There will be a thunderous ovation. Then the archbishop will advance before the kneeling prince and place the crown on his head. At that moment he will become the king.

There is a throne within your heart, and only you can say, "Lord Jesus, be Lord of all my life. I bow to Your authority and presence," and when that happens, the future becomes His responsibility. You can trust Him. He promised, "Never will I leave you; never will I forsake you" (Hebrews 13:5).

He is one King who always keeps His word.

In Closing

Take a pencil and jot down your thoughts which will bring the message of *Joyfully Single in a Couples' World* into focus in your life. I would also like to invite you to write to me and share any insights you have or thoughts I need to hear.

Before I read this book, I felt that . . .

I have come to see myself as . . .

As I look to the future, my goal is . . .

What I have learned about myself is that I . . .

With God's help, I will . . .

What I have most determined to change is . . .

Lord, thank You for helping me with . . .

You can write to

> Dr. Harold J. Sala
> *Guidelines* International
> Box G
> Laguna Hills, CA 92654
> E-mail: hsala@compuserve.com

Endnote

1. C.S. Lewis, "We Have No Right to Happiness," *The Saturday Evening Post*, April 1982, p. 44.

Also by Harold Sala:

Touching God: 52 Guidelines for Personal Prayer